WINTERS' TALES

RANDOM HOUSE
NEW YORK

JONATHAN WINTERS

WINTERS' TALES

STORIES AND OBSERVATIONS
FOR THE UNUSUAL

JONATHAN WINTERS 87

Library of Congress Cataloging-in-Publication Data

Winters, Jonathan.
Winters' tales.

I. Title.
PS3573.I545W56   1987   813'.54   84-42648
ISBN 0-394-56424-3

Manufactured in the United States of America

9

ILLUSTRATIONS BY JONATHAN WINTERS
DESIGNED BY JO ANNE METSCH

To
EILEEN, JAY, AND LUCINDA,
WHO LISTENED TO MY STORIES
OVER AND OVER AGAIN

To
GEORGE SPOTA,
WHO ENCOURAGED ME TO DO THIS BOOK

AND A THANKS TO
DAVID ROSENTHAL,
WHO GAVE ME A KEY TO RANDOM HOUSE

CONTENTS

vii

CONTENTS

ANIMAL TALES

CONTENTS

CONTENTS

INTRODUCTION

This book, the pieces of which I've written over the last twenty-five years, is for adults. But I hope, more than anything, that it also appeals to the child in all of us, the child we should always strive to nurture and preserve. I've worked hard on keeping the child in me alive, and perhaps this collection will help you do the same too. I hope so.

Maybe I should explain.

When I was a child, like most children, I had toys. Not a lot, but enough. Don't misunderstand. I know there are millions of children all over the world who not only had no toys, but also no pets or parents.

When the Depression hit in the thirties, almost all Americans lost their savings, their belongings, and their property and homes. So what toys I did have I cherished and really took care of. (I had my first electric train up to and through my marriage. In fact, my son had it for some time and later gave it to his cousin.)

After my parents were divorced in 1932, when I was seven, I went from Dayton to Springfield, Ohio, to live with my mother. The toys she gave me through grade school and on up to high school were sufficient; I can't complain. When I wanted my first bicycle (a lot of money in those days), I worked all summer on my grandfather's farm carrying water bottles. I finally earned enough, and bought one made by the Huffman Bicycle Company with balloon tires and red and black trim. This was the only bike I had till I moved out here to California in the early 1960s.

Though I had that bike a long time, there were very few other toys that I was able to keep. Why? Because they were given away while I was away during World War II. When I came home, like most boys or men, I went to my room to reminisce and go through my old goodies. But they weren't there; I asked my mother, "What happened to my toys?"

"Why, dear," she replied, "I gave them all to the children at the mission."

I was glad they had gone to poor kids, rest assured of that, but I said to my mother, "They weren't yours to give away. You should have written me because there were some things I had hoped to keep forever."

My mother answered, "But how did I know you would be coming home?"

Still, I do have my first baseball glove, a couple of children's books by Ernest Thompson Seton, my first wristwatch, an expensive watch my grandfather gave me one Christmas and a couple of medals I won in summer camp—that's about it for the old stuff. But I've been adding other toys. For instance, I recently collected all the major league baseball caps. Being a Cincinnati Reds fan, I have several baseballs and bats signed by the team, and a couple of Reds' shirts (authentic), the road version and the one they wear when they play at home. I also have an official shirt from the Yankees and a couple of baseballs signed by Hank Aaron after he beat Babe Ruth's home run record. Then I have many pairs of Indian moccasins from various tribes (and I wear them). I have a Hudson Bay robe the Black Foot of Montana gave me. And I wear all kinds of caps, hats and shirts, all kinds of costumes. (Many's the time I wear my strange outfits around my neighborhood or out of it. My wife has said to me, "You wonder why you get a lot of static? You're asking for it!")

I have my reasons for accumulating these toys, these other things: I genuinely enjoy having them. They've brought me a lot of joy and are *still* bringing me a lot of joy. Not that everyone responds well to this. It's amazing how many people I run into who say to me, "You're almost childlike; you act like a little boy." Only a few weeks ago a man about my age approached me; I had on my Cincinnati Reds warm-up jacket and cap.

"Hey, Winters," this clown said, "aren't you a little old to be wearing an outfit like that? Say, how old are you anyway?"

I told him I was sixty-one, and added, "Would you believe when *I* was *twelve*, I was sixty-one?"

Over the years I've found so many men, men I've known and not known, who were really uptight about acting like a little boy or being a little boy. They were afraid of being judged. But to me, the same man who criticizes a grown man for being a little boy is the guy who puts on a lamp shade when he's bombed. He's the same man who at fifty years of age drops a paper bag full of water on the people walking on the street below or pulls a chair out from under a guest at a dinner party. I always find that it's the wrong people who ask, "Aren't you ever going to grow up?"

Now, there's no question about it, a hell of a lot of people—men and women alike—don't ever grow up, not one bit. But why can't you be both when you're middle-aged—a man *and* a little boy? When it comes time to be a man, be a man. When it comes time to be a little boy, don't sweat it, *be* a little boy.

The lesson is this: Hold on to your toys, especially if they mean a lot to you. Many will be lost or broken, some you'll give away, but always hold on to a few if you can. Take it from me, a sixty-one-year-old boy. It's fun to open that old chest or push back that antique rolltop desk and leaf through some of those yellowing pictures, pull out those letters you won in football or baseball in high school, that spinning top you used, marbles, the uniform you wore in the service, the medals you won or whatever they are. I remember my stepfather, who, while in his mid-sixties, came across the old teddy bear that he had when he was a little boy. From then on, until the day he died, it sat on the corner of *his* rolltop desk. There was something warm and wonderful about a man six foot six and sixty-seven years old gazing up at his teddy bear.

What happened to my toys? Why, I got them back,

not all of them by a long shot. I pointed out that I didn't have that many to begin with, but the tops I have now are more fun to play with than ever before. I hope to grow to be an old man, and I hope that instead of putting the newspaper in my lap I would have a "teddy bear."

Where are or what happened to your toys? I hope if you're my age (or even younger), you've still got a few things left from your childhood. I was just thinking: wouldn't it be neat if there were a big toy store with only kids' toys in it but all the toys would be for us adults, not the kids?

Throughout my life, I've been gratified that I've been able to keep the child in me alive and inspire others to do the same. If these stories do that for you, I'll be happy. (Or maybe I should say *happier*.) Not all of these tales, of course, are funny, but I hope they all let you use your imagination in whatever way that sets you free. It's what they've done for me, and if I'm lucky, they will do the same for you, too.

Not long ago, my daughter, Lucinda, wrote a poem for me on the occasion of my sixtieth birthday. I'm very proud of her, always have been, but what touched me most about her words was what she said about how I taught her to be fearless about doing whatever she felt truly expressed her real self, to be "proud to be strange." I think her words are especially appropriate now.

My Special Friend

I can picture you fifty years ago and more playing alone,

Creating invisible friends, speaking their dialogues, acting each role.

I'm a lot like you.

I played alone with fantasy characters, questioned my vivid imagination,

But you taught me not to be afraid to be alone or unusual.

You taught me to be proud to be strange.

I can picture you as an old man with still the imagination of a child,

And me, a middle-aged woman mentally and spiritually playing alongside.

Two special friends, two children, an unusual father and his unusual daughter.

WINTERS'
TALES

UNUSUAL
STORIES

THE ARTIST

Even as a little boy, Alexander Brooks excelled as an artist. At the tender age of seven he was already showing promise and competed with seniors in high school. His parents, unfortunately, did little or said little to encourage Alex. But his grandfather, his father's father, who had once been a half-assed painter, egged him on.

When he was graduated from prep school, Alex received honors. And although, at his father's insistence, he studied to become a lawyer, young Alex made a point of also taking a minor in fine arts in college.

After finishing law school, Alexander was expected

to join his father's law firm as a partner. But before he began work there, Alex was given a trip around the world as a present from his grandfather. He went around the world, all right, but instead of going to see his grandfather upon his return, Alexander Brooks disappeared into thin air. Unbeknownst to his father, Alex wanted to be an artist all along.

With little or no income, the life of an artist is without a doubt terribly frustrating. And though Alex was a fine painter, he found himself continuing to live in one room. He had no heat in the winter, zero social life, a constant itching sensation, a fake TV set and half a bottle of wine. A number of Alex's pieces were scattered around the room, and a large array of half-finished canvases was randomly stacked along with stretcher bars. His career was going nowhere and he was unhappy.

Alex had never really gotten along with his father, barely tolerated his mother and, overall, had become pretty disenchanted with the "system." He was like a lot of young (and old) people, full of hostility and finding it hard to release it. But one day he finally figured a way to get his feelings out. Since his paintings weren't selling that well anyway and a lot of good people couldn't afford his works, he'd take it upon himself to go to them! And he did.

When he sold his first large painting for thirty-five hundred dollars, he took this money to the local hardware store and purchased every spray can in every color available, put all the cans in a huge carton and took them back to his room.

He was not the kind of person to destroy, mar or deface anybody's property, but his bitter quarrels with his father had slowly evolved into hatred. He decided he would now strike back at his father, and the system, by spray-painting everything they stood for.

Alex, deep down inside, was hurting and was also very ashamed of what he was about to do. He even hated spray cans. Nonetheless, Alex set out to deface every prominent edifice in the city. He had to work very carefully, or he'd be spotted by the authorities. He would spray at night. Holidays were good and even rainy days. He painted in the wee hours of the morning and on Sundays, which for the most part seemed best of all. He never used any off-color language, but he would spray people and animals doing the damnedest things. Being a virtual recluse, he saw nobody and nobody saw him.

One day, while he was making one of his rare visits to the grocery store, he encountered a large crowd. There were at least a thousand people and they were all looking up at the side of the First National Bank

Building. Alex immediately recognized one face in the crowd as his father's. Because Alex was wearing his artist's costume, a wild item that was a little bit of everything, including a black beret and a huge pair of shades, he wasn't recognized as he made his way swiftly through the crowd to where his father was standing.

A local television crew was filming the artwork on the bank. It was Alex's work. He had used every color out of every spray can available. It was really, he thought, the best graffiti he'd ever done. The subject matter was five men and five women holding up the bank. They were all wrapped in American flags, creating a lot of symbolism.

Alex's father's office was on the top floor of the bank. The father told the television reporter he was thoroughly shocked by the defacing of *any* building, but he did think that this particular work was "most unusual," extremely "patriotic," and "should be preserved." He also pointed out that it was a shame that the young man or woman who did this work was unknown; he made a plea on television that the artist come forward and receive a special award and a check for five thousand dollars. Before signing off, the television reporter said that when the individual did surface, he or she would not be punished, and that the work, according to the "city fathers" (Alex's father was a member of that board), would be preserved for all time.

Late that night Alex went back to the building and added this signature: "Alexander Brooks—born 1940, died 1980."

I MISS DANCING
WITH YOU

I miss dancing with you—feeling your cheek next to mine. Looking into your eyes—holding you ever so close. Hoping the orchestra will never stop playing and pretending all along that it was just us on that big floor, sort of like Astaire and Rogers.

I miss dancing with you because for those few hours I felt you were mine. People don't dance like we used to. Our music said something—the lyrics, the words, the singers, the musicians; everything blended into one incredibly beautiful evening. We all looked good—so clean, so innocent; every cent I had went into that evening. God, it was worth it, just knowing I'd be dancing with you!

You always looked so pretty—I know you didn't have a lot of dresses, but you made them look different. I always felt so dumb in the same dark suit. The only thing that made my clothes different was my tie—I always had about six different ties.

I miss dancing with you—that perfume you wore—how many times we'd bump into another couple and the girl or the guy would say, "Gosh, what is that perfume you're wearing!" You'd laugh and say, "Don't you remember? I work at the perfume counter at Rike's?"

I miss dancing with you because it was never just another dance—it was like the great ball in the greatest ballroom, held only once a year and only for very special people. You were special—you're still special. How proud I was to have you as my partner for all the dances. Every guy on the floor couldn't keep his eyes off you as we turned this way and that. Even the girls would remark, "She is incredibly beautiful, isn't she?"

Oh God, I miss dancing with you! Why did it have to stop? Hell, you know as well as I do—it's 'cause I paid you to dance with me. I have no regrets—nobody ever saw my left sleeve was empty. Who would dance with a one-armed guy? Wherever you are, you'll be happy to know I finally got an arm, but I still miss dancing with you.

When I look back, you were wrong, you know, to charge me for all those dances. But I guess it's all kind of worked out. Mom wrote me that you and your husband were at the symphony, in the front row, and that somehow the harp fell over on you and broke your back.

You know something. I still miss dancing with you.

STOLEN FLOWERS

A thief is a thief. Nobody likes a thief, except perhaps for Robin Hood. And while stealing anything is unforgivable, stealing flowers is *unheard* of. Why steal flowers when so many of them bloom in the world, in open fields, forests, canyons, deserts, around rivers, lakes and oceans? At least that's what I thought until I first saw the "flower thief" a few years ago.

I was at the florist's, buying a bouquet for a lady friend of mine who was hospitalized for some minor surgery. While I waited, the thief took four red roses and stuffed them under his filthy raincoat. I could have reported him, but didn't. I wanted to catch him. I paid for my bouquet, and I followed him.

He was walking rapidly along the main street, then darted down one alley and then another and still another. I saw him go up to a small run-down home that had two window boxes with some bright red geraniums in them. He smelled each one slowly, like a bee visiting a flower. Suddenly he stopped smelling the flowers and let out a dreadful cry, a distorted roar. The geraniums were plastic!

All this time, the four roses he had stolen were still tucked under his raincoat. I was convinced that they must have wilted.

Whom was the thief taking the flowers to? Though I lost him momentarily, I found him again, placing one of his red roses on the windshield of an abandoned ambulance. He next headed to a public park that at one time had been beautiful but was now strewn with trash, cans, bottles, and all kinds of debris. Amid this garbage in a stone path was an old drunk lying on what used to be a World War II Army coat. The thief approached the drunk, bent over slowly and placed his second rose on the bum's chest. The rose almost appeared alive again as the bum kept breathing ever so slowly.

The thief suddenly began to run fast; it was hard to keep up with him. When he finally stopped, it was in front of a gay bar that had been not only closed but boarded up and condemned with a huge homemade sign that read: AIDS. He took a thumbtack out of the sign, stuck it through the stem of his third rose and nailed it against the sign.

Before I knew it, he turned around and got on a bus; at the last minute I got on, too. After almost forty-five minutes the bus stopped at the V.A. cemetery. The thief got off and I stealthily continued to follow him at a distance. After passing row after row of crosses, he stopped, knelt gently and put his last rose on one of the graves. He got up, stood quietly for a while, then let out a scream and began stealing all the flowers he could from other graves, gathering them up in his arms.

Now I ran after him and tackled him. No sooner had we both hit the ground than I looked around me and saw behind every stone or cross a young man in his military uniform standing at attention. It was the most frightening experience I've ever had. In unison their voices said, "Let him alone, let him alone, we all stole flowers too!" They then all broke into song, a war song I'd never heard. As quickly as it had started, it all ended as they abruptly disappeared, including the thief I had been following. I was all alone in the huge veterans' cemetery.

How I made my way back to my home that evening I'll never know. When I did arrive home, it was just before dark and my wife and two children were huddled together in front of the house. I couldn't believe my eyes! Except for the front door and the windows on the first and second stories, our home was completely covered with flowers.

"Thank God, John, you're home!" my wife said. "Look! Look at our home!" She was hysterical. The children were crying.

"There must've been a thousand of them putting flowers all over the front of the house," she continued. "Just as we started into the driveway, they finished, burst into song and then they all drove away in florist's vans. What's it all about, John? John, what the hell is going on? Why would they do this to our house? Why are you wearing your Marine uniform?"

THE WEDDING

The interior of the church was magnificent. The huge, beautiful stained-glass windows were unique. Lighted candles were everywhere about the altar and the sides, plus two very large candles that were every bit of two feet in height. The place was filled to capacity.

It was *the* big wedding of the year and many famous people were there. All through the service I kept saying to myself: Gosh, I can't wait to see what they got for presents." With a wedding this size and this many important and wealthy people attending, these two newlyweds would never have to worry about furnishing their house. I was just glad to be an usher. Woody, the bridegroom, and I had been friends in college, really close friends. His family had a lot of money; mine was tapped out.

Woody's bride, Eileen, was probably the most beautiful girl I'd ever seen. And she was just as beautiful inside. In our last year at school, Woody had been the best jock on campus and Eileen was Homecoming Queen. It was all so perfect, and now, today, they were about to take their final vows, to become husband and wife.

I stood there at the altar and listened to the minister reading from his prayer book: "Will you take this woman to be your lawful wedded wife, in sickness and in health?" and so on. I couldn't help thinking, Here I am almost thirty-five and still single. What a bummer going back to that lousy apartment tonight after all this has ended. God! Will *they* be having fun tonight. Me? I'll just get out of this ridiculous morning suit and return it to the regular place.

Shortly before the ceremony came to a close, I looked across at one of Eileen's bridesmaids who was a knockout in her own right. Her name was Sarah Coolidge, and she had long jet-black hair and the biggest, most beautiful blue eyes I've ever seen anywhere. She smiled at me and I thought I saw her lips open momentarily, whispering, "I'll see you at the reception!" Maybe, just maybe, we could be falling in love and I could marry her next year. I'd never be alone again. We'd have, after a year or two, a little boy. Yeah! I've got to have a little boy. Being an only child, I've got to carry on the name. What name? I suddenly had to think, What the hell is my real name?

I looked around me, at all these people, the candles, the bride and bridegroom and the stained-glass windows. A deathly hush fell over the place and the assistant director yelled out, "Okay, gang, that's a *wrap*. Same place tomorrow, stage eleven. Pick up your call sheets on the way out."

As I was heading toward my dressing room, I said good-night to Woody, the bridegroom in this turkey. He didn't even acknowledge me; he sort of waved, that's all. His beautiful bride, Eileen, slipped her arm through that of some gray-haired clown's and they skipped across the stage past the soundman and through the exit. I was doing what I've been doing for years. I was already out of those ridiculous clothes and on my way back to my apartment.

THE HIJACKER

Outside, the thermometer read 150 below zero. Now, that's colder than Kelsey's you-know-what. Inside, though, it was snug and warm. There was a huge fire on the hearth and everybody was scurrying about finishing his project. The old gentleman with the rosy cheeks and unusually red nose was sitting in his rocking chair, slowly swaying back and forth. His sweet wife, who looked a lot like him, but, of course, wasn't sporting a beard, sat at his side as he smoked his long clay pipe and laughed quietly to himself.

All of his helpers were putting last-minute touches on toys they had been working on for months. Eleven

months. Outside were tiny reindeer, all huddled together, their big, soft brown eyes blinking from time
to time. They appeared ready to go, to circle the Earth
in less than twenty-four hours.

All of Santa's helpers, the "little people," as the old
gent called them, looked like a huge beltline as they
moved the toys from Santa's house to the sleigh,
which, finally, was filled to the brim. All the little
people formed a big circle around Santa, sang him a
Christmas carol and blew him a kiss. Then, just before
Saint Nick climbed into his sleigh, Mrs. Claus gave
him a big, big kiss on the cheek, saying, "Take care of
yourself, don't take any unnecessary chances, keep
your muffler about your throat and check all your
reindeer, look out for shooting stars, comets and anything else that may be out there." Santa snapped his
long black whip just above the reindeer and shouted,
"Up, up and away, here's hoping all those good little
boys and girls all over the world are fast asleep. Santa
is on his way."

Unknown to Santa was the fact that one of the
little people had hidden himself directly under his
sleigh by taping himself there. No sooner had Santa
and the reindeer climbed out of Mrs. Claus's sight,
well on their way with the North Pole only a speck
behind them, than the little person crawled up on

Santa's pack of toys. Though he was the same size as the other little people, he had a very grotesque face and an evil look. And as Santa made his way through the starry night toward Earth, the little person suddenly pulled from his jacket a six-cylinder handgun. He cocked it and said, "Turn around, you fat red-nosed old man, we're going to Saturn. You turn this sleigh around now or I'll kill you."

Santa, needless to say, was horrified, and for what seemed like an eternity he said nothing and looked straight ahead. He never was one to ask favors from anyone, but this was a special evening, with all the children waiting for all those presents. This was the most special night of the whole year. So he looked into the heavens and said, "Oh Lord, what am I to do?"

Abruptly, the dwarf pulled hard on Santa's cap. "Now, old man, turn this thing around, now!" he screamed. "You're not just dealing with a run-of-the-mill dwarf-brownie-helper here. When the Earth and all the boys and girls read about me on Christmas Day, I'll be the most famous little person in the world. I'm sick to death of being small. I'll be big, *big*, do you hear?"

He was about to get up on Santa's shoulder when from out of nowhere a long, thick icicle materialized and went right through the dwarf. Santa heard nothing, but felt a strong pull on his shoulder. As he turned around he saw frozen to his shoulder the dwarf's glove. He heaved a great sigh of relief. All the reindeer looked back at Santa and winked.

Then all of them looked down at Earth. Though they were still a long, long way up, it was as if the old world had been wrapped in a deep blue blanket with millions of diamonds placed on it. It was Christmas Eve and all the children would get their gifts, as promised. Santa chuckled as he remembered one of the toys just happened to be a hijacker doll.

A WELL-KEPT
SECRET

Ever since I was a little boy, I, Edward Wellington Marsh, was considered to be delicate. I was shy, rather pale in appearance, fairly tall, but definitely frail—rather effeminate-looking. As a boy, in grade school, up and through high school, I had very few friends. Actually, had it not been for Wayne Huffman I don't think I would've had any friends at all.

My father was rather short and stocky—the linebacker type—and as a matter of fact he had played a couple of years at Yale. He and I didn't hit it off from the start—everything he liked I didn't. I liked art, he loved golf, and he made me, as a kid, caddie.

My God, how I hated that game and still do! If you want to hear profanity for a couple of hours, watch cheating, and endure an endless lecture on the power of concentration, I guess it can be a fun game. He also liked to hunt—target practice after church on Sundays. I've always hated guns in any kind of game. They have always represented one thing to me, death. How well I remember Father making me go pheasant shooting with him. We didn't have any pointers or Labs, so I picked up the dead birds.

The only one I was really close to in the family was my grandfather—my father's father. My mother ran away with another man when I was three, so I never knew her at all—except that I hated her. Come to think of it, I hated women, period. What few women I did go out with in high school were nothing but teasers.

But Grandfather—Grandfather and I were, from the beginning, great friends. More than that, he loved me and I loved him. He once told me he'd wished I'd been his son instead of my dad.

My grandmother was very stiff, proper, carried herself well, a lovely aristocratic lady—but cold, very cold. She was constantly correcting me: when I sat down at the table to eat, she had me mind my manners; she told me to walk straight; to get up immediately when a lady came into the room, to open the door for her, to open the door to the house, to the car, to the restaurant, and so on. She'd make sure I'd dress correctly going to any function. And at all times I was to be a gentleman—never to gawk at a woman, or leer, and keep my hands to myself when I'd go out on a date.

God! As I look back I hated women! Everything had to be on their terms. Men could be that way, I know—but nothing like the women I had known.

Grandfather, on the other hand, was fun—loads of fun. He was tall, blue-eyed, with white hair. He had a fabulous sense of humor. James Thurber (a friend of his) once said of him: "For God's sake, Wells, if you start sending articles to *The New Yorker* or writing books on humor, I'd be out of work!" (My grandfather's nickname was "Wells"; his real name was Wellington Gaines Marsh. I guess for some odd reason my great-grandfather's idol was the Duke of Wellington. I have no idea why.)

It was after Grandmother died in the late 1930s that I really got to know Grandfather. He had been a very successful banker, was president of the most respected bank in town, but with the crash of 1929, the bank went under like so many thousands of others across the nation. But he was a survivor and had fortunately saved enough to maintain the old house and to hold on to his car and occasionally make a few trips to New York to kick up his heels.

He *loved* women—found them to be much more fun and interesting than men. He loved to dance, and once he was a widower, a bachelor again, he leaped at the chance to go to dances. After Grandmother died he began to date almost immediately. When I was a senior in high school, he'd had a few shooters and told me how lovely Grandmother was, how she was truly one of the town's great beauties, but like so many great beauties was cold as ice. Grandfather craved affection and needed desperately to be loved. I felt the same thing—I needed to be loved, too. When it came right down to it, with Dad gone most of the time out on the road as a salesman, it was just Grandfather and me.

World War II broke out, and I enlisted in the Navy —at age sixteen. Grandfather forged Dad's signature, thank God! The Navy never found out; I don't think they would have done much to me, just chewed me out and sent me home, but Grandfather might've gone to jail. Anyway, I was in the Navy for only six months; they sent me home with a medical discharge, labeling me a latent homosexual with strong leanings toward being a conscientious objector. The final straw was when I was caught wearing a Wave uniform during a leave.

Rather than go home after being discharged, I decided to live in San Francisco, where I had spent three of the six months of my unusual Navy career. Here I could dress in drag—be a queen—even come out of the closet as a full-blown homosexual. This was the life I'd wanted all along.

I continued to write to Grandfather and tell him I was aboard a destroyer, as a gunner's mate (how butch can you get?) and would return probably in a year. Actually, I went to work in the top gay club in San Francisco, Quaranta Uno.

It was here that all the young men and a few old queens did two shows nightly in full drag. And they were stunning! These young men had come from all over the world to appear in this particular club because its reputation was the best for what it offered. I stayed on at the club for a couple of years, having one love affair after another. I even dated one girl, a very pretty waitress named Emily. She unfortunately tried desperately to change me and, of course, I laughed at her.

One night, while bombed out of my mind, I really roughed her up. Before leaving her tiny apartment, I took her lipstick and wrote on her bathroom mirror: "You bitches are all the same—you suck!"

All this time I continued to write to Grandfather, who was then close to eighty-five years of age and living in a boardinghouse. My father knew nothing about all this and probably couldn't have cared less.

I decided I would move to Las Vegas—I was getting on in years myself. I landed myself a job as one of the chorus (I was no longer a headliner) at the big and only gay revue in Vegas, The Cats. I decided to write my grandfather in hopes he would come out and see me. I knew the old man could go any minute and desperately wanted to see him one more time. All he knew was what I'd written him: that I was out of the Navy and had become a maître d' in Vegas. I sent the old man a round-trip plane ticket, plus some cash. I told him I'd be away in Los Angeles for a couple of days, but to go to the club where the girls are, The Cats, and to ask for Lilly Long. He was to come to her room, number 11, after the last show.

I explained that Lilly was a knockout, especially for someone of thirty-eight. I told my grandfather he'd flip out over Lilly and that, given his love for the ladies, he'd have the time of his life—or what's left of it—if he went home with her.

Well, the old man got the letter, the tickets and the money and, needless to say, was reborn. He got into Vegas, checked in at a small hotel and decided to miss the first floor show so he could rest up for the second to see Lilly. I, of course, readied myself in my dressing room for the second show and was on a natural high, waiting to see what this old grandfather of mine would think of Lilly. Sure enough, after the show, the old man came backstage and knocked on number 11. A dirty old man is a dirty old man, but my grandfather, Wellington Gaines Marsh, had class.

Grandfather, looking every bit of eighty-five, was still very thin and trim; he was wearing a dark pin-striped suit and, I noticed, a really good white rug. He stood at my dressing room, number 11, and knocked ever so gently. I had changed into a stunning deep green velvet dress, and was wearing diamond earrings, a beautiful blond wig and just a suggestion of makeup. I was, for all intents and purposes, a very beautiful middle-aged lady, not just a chorus girl and certainly not an ordinary stripper. I opened the door slowly and there stood my grandfather.

"Do come in, Mr. Marsh—I *do* call you Mr. Marsh, don't I?"

The old man just stood there, gawking, his old, withered right hand grasping a fresh bouquet of violets.

"You may call me Wells, Miss Long," he said,

blushing. "My real name is Wellington Gaines Marsh."

"You call me Lilly, Wells! Do come in—I have just a few things to pick up and I want to make one call to check on our reservations. I've picked a divine place to eat about twenty miles outside of Vegas—I do hope you like French food."

The old man's mouth was half open. After what seemed like an hour he finally spoke. "Edward is my grandson and I understand that you've been friends for some time—how fortunate he is to know a lovely lady like yourself. It's my understanding he'll be back from Los Angeles in a few days. I must confess I can't wait to see him, it's been a number of years, he's been more like my own boy. He's remembered all of my birthdays, and God knows I've had a lot of 'em. And he's never forgotten to send me presents at Christmas and a silly Valentine on Valentine's Day. How's he enjoying being a maître d'? With his charm he'll own that hotel someday! Oh, I'm sorry, here I've been rambling and rambling, forgive an old man—especially a lonely old man!"

"Oh, don't be silly, Wells, I understand completely. I want to get to know you, everything about you. Edward said to look after you, you were his favorite person. I assure you we're going to have a very, very special evening. Incidentally, I hope you don't think I'm being too forward if I ask you to stay over at my place? The restaurant we're going to is about twenty miles out of town and to drive all the way back into this Neon Nightmare is sort of silly. I have a lovely guest room, a little frilly; Edward stays there every once in a while when he's depressed, or just wants to get away from people and the crowds around the slots. This place *does* get on your nerves when you have to be here all year round! Well, Wells, shall we have a go at it?"

The old man responded: "Lilly, my arm, either one is yours. *I'm* yours."

The little French place was quiet, neat, and not too expensive. Grandfather naturally insisted on paying the bill, but Lilly just winked at the owner. And off we drove to my—Lilly's—apartment.

My house was a small adobe ranch-type home that I'd bought shortly after I got to Las Vegas. It was about as feminine a home as one would expect—big fluffy pillows everywhere and a Seeburg jukebox with loads of records in it (it worked—a collector's piece). There were a few Early Colonial chests and chairs scattered here and there, plus a couple of Navajo rugs on the floor and an antique hat rack with all kinds of wild ladies' hats on it. Nearby was a beautiful Spanish mirror in the living room, all hand-carved with a gold finish, given to me by some star I was on the bill with somewhere. The bed, a huge four-poster done in solid cherry, had matching night tables done in tiger maple dating back to about 1850.

There were lots of pictures of me as Lilly and one of me when I was Edward in the Navy. There were also a number of women in different-sized frames who, when you looked at them closely, had very short hair and clothes that were more than a little masculine.

When we arrived, I entered first, with the old man following. "I guess I'm supposed to say about this time, 'Forgive, me, Wells, the place is a mess!' But as you can see, it's anything but that—I'm really neat as a pin!—I hate to come home to a messy house! Don't you agree, Wells?"

"Oh, yes, my dear—a woman of your beauty and elegance deserves only the best," replied the old man.

"Can I fix you something to drink," I asked, "perhaps a glass of white wine while I slip into something more comfortable?"

Wells said, "I've already had two drinks at dinner,

one more just might put me out of action altogether. Oh, what the hell, Lilly. It's like Edward always says, 'Go for it!' "

In a matter of minutes I came out to sit beside Grandfather on a lovely old love seat I'd purchased up in Carson City. Slowly I put my arm around the old man. What was flashing through my mind was, It's true that this is my grandfather and the old man hasn't the foggiest idea his grandson is sitting next to him and is about to kiss him.

Slowly, ever so slowly, I put down my glass of wine and took his glass from him and put it on the coffee table in front of us. I slowly took his hand and turned the old man's face toward mine. I began to kiss my grandfather—wildly, moving my lips around, over, in. I even stuck my tongue in the old man's mouth.

What went through my mind was incredible: a series of flashbacks, going back to the time I was a little boy sitting on my grandfather's lap, my grandfather kissing me on the cheek after telling me a bedtime story; I remembered kissing my grandfather when he was laid up for several weeks when he had tried to play softball at the Fourth of July picnic; when I went off to join the Navy it was my grandfather who kissed me good-bye at the train station.

And now I was Lilly! How long I was kidding the

old man is anybody's guess. Suddenly I got up. "Forgive me, Wells, I must visit the powder room." I came out a moment later wearing just a robe; I stood there looking at the old man. How much I loved my grandfather over the years. And now it had come down to this. Should I tell him the truth? Lay it all out there? It would break the old man's heart. I kept saying over and over to myself: "Why, in God's name did I ever send for this wonderful old man? What the hell *did* I have in mind. Son of a bitch!"

The old man turned around and gave an unusual look to Lilly. "You know, my dear," Wells said, "in all my eighty-five years I've kissed a lot of women, but *you're* the best! I mean that. Damn it to hell, I wish I was sixty-five again—I'd show you one hell of a good time."

I smiled, started toward him, and caught my robe's belt on the edge of the sofa. It fell to the floor and curled like a snake about my feet. I stood naked, stark naked.

The old man was hard of hearing, had arthritis in both hands, a slight limp hampered his walk, but his eyesight was that of a man of forty. He sat dumbfounded, looking at what was obviously male anatomy —and well-endowed male anatomy at that. Grandfather grabbed his chest, obviously in incredible pain, gave a few short gasps, then managed to get out, "*Why me?*" He slumped over and died.

In going through my grandfather's wallet, I came across a picture of myself in a Wave uniform. A pal (a gay pal) of mine had gotten the old man's address and sent the picture to him, attaching a vicious note saying, "This is your *real* grandson." I guess Grandfather never really bought it, but instead believed it to be strictly another example of my far-out sense of humor.

A ROLL
IN THE HAY

From time to time when I was a little boy, I was always goin' in and outa Grandpaw's big red barn. Year-round it was filled with hay. There were always some horses in their stalls, a few chickens runnin' in and around the farm machinery, some hand tools, bridles, a couple of rusty buckets, a big cracked pot, sacks of feed and a couple of rakes with the handles missin'.

One hot August day—back when I was a freshman in high school—me and Sissy MacGregor, the girl who lives two farms away from us, was up in the loft; we was both packin' hay to get some extra money.

And my God, it was hot—hotter than a burnt boot. The sweat was really rollin' down our faces. The only air come our way was when them pigeons would fly in and out of the barn.

After a while, me and Sissy both commenced to get thirsty; as I reached over to grab a jug of water, a barn owl made a pass over me—guess he'd seen a mouse in the hay. It sure scared us, but then Sissy and I was laughin' and rollin' around up in that loft. Guess we all heard that expression "A roll in the hay"? Well, pretty soon I come to get excited and tried to pull her pants down. I 'bout had 'em off when I lost my footing and fell against a pitch fork, which hit Sissy, who fell clean outa the loft and landed on Grandpaw, who was countin' nails into a fruit jar. She hit him such a good lick he ain't never *talked* since. Sissy incidentally weighed close to three hundred pounds.

When she did get off Grandpaw, she took off like a bat outa hell. We never have seen her since. Her mom claimed she dyed her hair and is livin' in another part of the state with a blind man.

THE CONDUCTOR

The first sound Winston P. Larch of Ludlow, Kentucky, can remember is the sound of a locomotive. Winston was all of five years of age when he heard that whistle, growing up during the great Depression in the poorest section of Ludlow, which bordered on the Ohio River across from Cincinnati. Winston's father was a section hand who worked the tracks and gravel beds of the Pennsylvania Railroad. Winston's mother took in washing and ironing, mostly of the only wealthy family in Ludlow, the Ungerlighters, a very prosperous German family who had meat plants in Kentucky and Ohio.

Most boys his age wanted to be a train's engineer,
but not Winston. Ever since he could recall, Winston
wanted to be a conductor. What railroad didn't
matter. He liked people, young and old alike, made
friends easily, and had what friends called an "incredible personality." And so in his second year in
high school he dropped out and applied for a job as
a fireman on the New York Central out of Cincinnati.

After only a few years he found himself in a blue-
black coat, shiny trousers, a round railroad cap and
black shoes. He had his own ticket puncher, too, and
last, but not least, his first "railroad" watch—a gold-
filled Hamilton, a gift from Mr. Ungerlighter, the
wealthy old German whose clothes his mother washed.

Winston was to work on the railroad as a conductor up and through World War II. He started
with the New York Central, then signed on with
the Norfolk & Western, ending up with his very own
diamond stickpin and another gold-filled watch while
being a conductor for the Santa Fe.

His last night on the Santa Fe was ghastly. The
Super Chief was highballing from Los Angeles, and
they were some two hours out. Winston, now an old
man with snow-white hair and bordering on senility,
was doing his usual duties. As he was punching tickets
he started to hear whimpering, muted sobbing and a

couple of loud cries. Then there was screaming. As he turned around to face the carful of passengers, he saw men, women and children with their hands over their heads—all the hands had large holes punched through the fingernails of the right thumbs. The career of Winston P. Larch, who had been a good, responsible, loyal conductor for three major railroads, thus came to a tragic close.

The only thing that kept him from a jail sentence was his plea of senility. But when he left the courthouse in Chicago that snowy day back in 1945, the people on that train that night jumped him and punched holes in all his nails on both of his hands.

When he put his hands to his face he could see tiny holes of light, an act that illustrated the phrase "I see the light at the end of the tunnel."

BLACK TIE

Oh, God! do I have to put that damn thing on again? You women at least get a chance to wear a different-color dress, different shoes. I feel like a damn penguin, and when I enter the room, there, in the middle of all those people, is Admiral Byrd. He snaps his fingers and all of us men huddle about him like a huge gathering of those little black birds he saw in the Antarctic. No, thank you. No, thank you. Sorry, I just had some. Think I'll hold off until we sit down for the main course. Please, try these hors d'oeuvres, they're delicious. (That's the first half hour of dialogue.)

Look, there's the ambassador from Bolivia—what a toad. And his wife—who cares if she's an American, she's a toad, too.

What is this benefit all about?

Oh! There's Mrs. Woodrow Finch. What a stunning figure, considering she's every bit of eighty.

Anybody know who's entertaining us tonight? If it's one of those rock musicians or some goddamn country-western group, I'm out of here.

I can't believe what I'm seeing, that's the under secretary of state and he's throwing up on that rubber plant. I hope he doesn't do this when he goes abroad.

Have I told you, my dear, you're a knockout this evening, but do use this mouth spray. Better yet, here's a Life Saver. Your breath is foul.

What did you say? Two long black hairs coming out of my nose? Which nostril?

Look! Over there near the fireplace—that tall, thin young man. He's not wearing any shoes. My God, he's painted his feet black. Who *is* he? The secretary of labor's oldest son?

This dark man? Oh yes, he's the new toast of the art world. I understand he's going to be endorsed by the president. I know, I know, he's from India, Agra or Kashmir. Well, I don't care *how* gifted he is, he just cut one!

Would you believe it, I've already lost one of my gold cuff links. Dammit, they were two-and-a-half-dollar gold pieces. I hate these damn affairs. I'm always losing something!!

Who the hell is throwing this bash, anyway. Let's fight our way through this mess. You say you've got a sore throat and I'll tell him I'm leaving the first thing in the morning for the Mayo Clinic. They're going to run a study on my midlife crisis.

Do you know what that man and woman said to me? That bastard, the nerve of him. He said, "Would you be a good fellow and run around back and pick up my black Jag, the one with the seal of the United States on the door?" I told you when we left the house, these damn tuxedos are a real pain in the ass.

I'm sure you did get a lot of compliments on your dress. You should, it was a thousand dollars just to take it in.

It just dawned on me . . . we came with the Cross-rights and they left an hour ago. I tell you what, you stand on that side of the door and I'll stand on this side, facing you, and say good night to everybody and see how many of these numb-numbs will know if we're the host and hostess.

Good night, yes! yes! So glad you could come. You both look fantastic. We'll do it again, soon. Next year, probably at the Pavillon. Great to see you. . . .

Did Skip get into Yale? Oh God, that's neat. We've got one boy at Annapolis and the other at West Point and our daughter finished up at Smith. She's about to marry a very nice man who is the curator of the museum in Lisbon. He's fifty-eight, but he does know his art.

Let's get the hell out of here, darling. That white-haired man just kissed me on the cheek. Didn't he just take over as chairman of the board of Pan Am? No wonder the damn airline is up for grabs.

All right! All right! I'm doing my best to get a cab. I hailed that one, but that black cabbie gave me the finger. I tell you these tuxedos are not low profile. We could cut through the park, but being dressed like this, we'd get the hell beaten out of us for sure. Aw! A cab at last.

"Cabbie, 1600 Pennsylvania Avenue, please."

THE KING WHO
HAD TO BE QUEEN TOO

Many, many years ago in tiny Nokando, high in the Himalayas near Tibet, lived a remarkable king and his subjects. Because almost a thousand years ago a terrible plague killed off all the women except one, all but one of his subjects were men. The only female was a very, very old withered and ugly woman, who, because she couldn't have children, was told to live in an abandoned cave outside the village.

King Nokando, in his middle age, was a handsome figure of a man. The tallest man in his kingdom, he was almost six feet. He could read and write, was exceptionally good in higher mathematics and fencing, a crack shot with a pistol or a rifle, a shoemaker, a very good chef who could make over fifty different dishes, and an excellent repairer of watches—but he was very lonely because he had no queen. Down through the years he would send for women through his many catalogs of *Ladies of the World*. But none of them arrived, either because they couldn't stand the freezing weather conditions and the high altitude or because when they came within sight of Nokando they panicked and fled.

The king's male subjects lived on a strange diet of mountain goat, mountain goat cheese, a kind of wild lettuce, strong soup made from yak tail and, of course, large amounts of saltpeter to keep their sexual desires in check. These men were relatively happy, since they always had lots of chores to do and were busy with handicrafts they would sell to American tourists when they came once a year. But they too were concerned about their king not having a consort. And so they held a big assembly and decided that a small party should leave Nokando in search of a queen.

In the meantime the king went through all his closets and came across some marvelous women's robes, wigs and makeup. Most of these had long ago belonged to the ugly old woman who lived in the abandoned cave on the outskirts of the village. Unbeknownst to his subjects, the king began to wear the women's clothes, right after breakfast and right after dinner at night.

This behavior went on for years, certainly for as long as the queen's search party was gone. The consort was ultimately found in the province of Chow Mein: she was draped over a crashed single-engine aircraft, hanging out of the cockpit. She was barely alive. The men nursed her back to health; she was beautiful, blue-eyed, blond, just twenty-seven, from Middle America. She had been on her way around the world to write a book when her plane went down.

The men told her they had a proposition. Since she was without an airplane, her publishing house back in the States had cut off her funds and the Pepsi Corporation, which had sponsored her, didn't know of her whereabouts, she said she would become the queen. "Go for it!" she said.

The party of men from Nokando set out with the lady. Oh, wouldn't the king be happy at long last!

When the party arrived, the king married the blond pilot. They had their honeymoon in Middle America and then returned to the kingdom of Nokando. The blond pilot lady was now queen and all was well. Or so it seemed. It turned out that just before the king's party of men and the blond aviatrix arrived in Nokando, the king visited a nuclear power plant in India because he wanted to improve his kingdom's lighting. When the king came home, he had his annual check-up. The Nokando doctors were shocked to find that the king had developed a little problem because of his visit to the power plant.

After a year or two of marriage the queen found out the king was firing blanks. So now the king of Nokando is in the cave on the edge of the village living with the old lady whose clothes he used to wear.

THE FACE-LIFT

I've never been what you'd call handsome, certainly no Steve Stunning. No chance of ever replacing Clark Gable, Robert Redford or Paul Newman. Here I am just barely sixty and, well, talk about the power of suggestion. First my wife added her two cents: "John, those circles under your eyes are now bags. I can live with the crow's-feet at the sides of your eyes, but what a world of difference just a little plastic surgery would make. And the important thing is *you'll* feel so much better.

Next, an old friend of mine, a guy who's always

kept his age to himself, mentioned after a tennis match that he thought I'd aged a bit.

Then a young gal, a waitress, I bump into from time to time at a hamburger joint in the neighborhood asked me point-blank, "Mr. Harshman, how old are you? I know it's nosy of me, so you don't have to tell me if you don't want to!" I said I was sixty— turned sixty just last November. She smiled her usual broad grin and said, "Gosh! I mean you don't look it, but then I'll bet you've had a face job, right? Being in front of the public eye as much as you are and all." On my way back home, right then and there, I decided I'd have a face job.

How long would it take? How long would I have to have the bandages on? How long would I have to be in seclusion? Should I just hang around the house or would it be better to take a real trip, an interesting trip to a faraway place? Cost never entered my mind, I had plenty of money. The only person I wanted to know about it was Clara, my wife. I definitely didn't want anybody else to know—*nobody*.

Monday morning I contacted the best plastic surgeon on the Western seaboard. We spent the better part of a luncheon and a couple of extra hours in his office going over "what to expect." Well, I went ahead with it. Dr. Cane did my eyes, under the lids, erased the crow's-feet. He took some "tucks" under the chin, even wiped out some small blemishes on my nose and eliminated some deep worry lines in my forehead. After my face started to heal a bit, I took two weeks and went to a city I thought would be interesting but above all a place where nobody would know me—Quebec.

When I came home, even just pulling up our driveway, I confess I felt like a new man, a younger man. I drove the car into the garage and noticed the other car was gone; knowing my wife, I gathered she was out "antiquing" or looking for a piece of unusual jewelry. As I opened the door, Crackers, our old dog, barked and barked, and finally bit me. I had to kick his butt out. That old bastard actually bit me! And then Whiskers, our four-year-old cat, sprang and landed on my back as I was headed up the stairs. First the dog, then the cat. I never did have too many friends, but I had always considered Crackers and Whiskers two of the most important creatures in my life. I was afraid to think what Clara's reaction was going to be when she arrived home.

I thought I'd fix myself a drink, so I went down to the den. As I was mixing a scotch and soda I thought of our parrot, Long John. Every time I took the cover off his cage he would squawk, "Hello, John." I went over to his cage and pulled off the cloth cover. He turned his back on me—that's right—he turned his back on me! I decided right then and there I'd get good and drunk—this was one lousy homecoming.

When I woke up I was lying on the couch in our den. The parrot was still there in his cage. And at the edge of the couch were Crackers and Whiskers. As I blinked my eyes into focus, I saw some lady bending over me, yelling, "Wake up, you bastard. How dare you stretch out on my husband's couch, you drunken sot! I don't know who you are, but get the hell out of here—he's due home today!" I looked up at her and let her have it. "How dare you talk to me this way, you bitch—get lost. My wife is not a big lady, but she can deck you!" The animals began to bark and meow, and the parrot was cackling something fierce. One thing I hadn't bargained for—Clara had had a *face-lift*, too. And here we were, complete strangers.

TABLE FOR TWO

It was autumn in Venice. We were in our early forties and celebrating some twenty-two years of marriage. Though we had traveled a fair amount around the world, we'd never been to Venice. And now we were there. Never mind the chill in the air, or that it had been raining off and on; when you're in love and celebrating an anniversary, you don't mind the weather.

One afternoon shortly after two o'clock we decided to have lunch in a lovely little Italian café known as Il Piccolo on the canal not far from St. Mark's Square. The sun had finally come out, so we decided to eat out on the terrace. The scene was lively, colorful; there was an arts festival under way and artists young and old had come from all over to participate; everyone was wearing some kind of costume.

Seated outdoors, we embraced the festivities, admiring the gondolas and watching a few large motorboats full of laughing, singing people hurrying past us. After a while, we gave our order to the waiter, a tall, thin man with a very bad complexion and terribly unattractive nose that was more like a beak.

He took his time but finally returned with two glasses and a bottle of white wine. He rubbed his long fingers on his filthy apron and headed back toward the kitchen. We never saw him again, but it didn't matter. We finished the bottle of wine and were feeling very mellow, sort of warmly gawking at each other, the same looks we gave each other some twenty-two years before.

All at once came the sound of gunfire and screams. We spun around to see I don't know how many people sprawled over tables and on the restaurant's marble floor. Two men with machine guns, wearing masks, stared at us, then crossed themselves and disappeared. We looked at each other numbly, shocked that we were still alive. It had to have been our costumes. A couple of artists dressed as a priest and a nun.

NIAGARA FALLS

It was a beautiful day. There wasn't a cloud in the sky as I slipped my old yellow rubber life raft into the river. Tucked away on the raft was my portable radio, which was already giving out with some of my old Dorsey favorites. I think Sinatra was singing. I had my cooler with some beer in it, a couple of six-packs and a big—I mean big—submarine sandwich. I gave the old raft a push and made my way out into the river.

If anybody knew the river and Niagara Falls, it was me and my brothers. All four of us at some time or other had been guides at the base of the falls aboard the *Maid of the Mist*. It would chug close to the falls for the tourists to get pictures, to hear the roar of the falls and, yes, sometimes to get soaked from the heavy mist.

We all used to play chicken in the very life raft I was in. We'd separately get into the raft and take it within fifty feet of the edge of the falls, gun the outboard motor and head back upstream. You weren't allowed to use the motor until the last minute. Sure, it was crazy. So is car racing, hang gliding, parachuting out of a plane, bullfighting, you name it, it's all a death wish. We blamed it on the fact we were just kids.

I was in the river today because I just wanted to be in the old raft one more time. I didn't have to prove anything. I was seventy-five years old.

I had intended on being no more than fifteen or twenty minutes in the river. As I guided the old raft out into the center I turned around to reach in the cooler for the submarine sandwich. Suddenly, there was a loud bang, like the crack of a rifle. The big yellow raft was shriveling up in front of me. I was being swept down the river; I knew I was going over the falls. Many times in high school, in college, we kids had jumped in the old raft, gone down to the edge, gunned that Evinrude at the last instant and headed

57

back upriver. Not today, though. It was as if the river were saying, Now you sorry bastard, today you belong to me!

Sure enough, I was swept over the falls and fell God knows how many feet to the rocks below. With the water pouring over me, my back broken, I looked up at the blue sky above, where there was a huge rainbow. That was all I remember, except for one other thing. An old biplane was skywriting and it had spelled out directly above me: *Drink Sparkletts.*

HALLOWEEN

It was two days before Halloween. And I was facing two of the toughest decisions one has to make for October 31: What am I going to be this year and where do I get my costumes? Above all, I always want to have the most *original* costume at the party.

So now I was walking along Sunset Boulevard window-shopping for a mask and a costume. I had a pretty good idea of what I wanted for my outfit. Many times I'll do something really bizarre to bring attention to myself, short of appearing in the nude or embarrassing an entire room and eliminating myself from society.

I decided I would dress as Adolf Hitler; only instead of the usual brown uniform, I would wear a pink outfit with a swastika on the armband. Why pink? Because many people, including novelists and historians, suggest that Hitler was a homosexual.

In any event, I purchased the costume. (Well, let's be honest; a friend of mine made it especially for me.) Now I had to find the mask. All day I went from store to store, trying to find a mask that might even be close to what Hitler looked like. Finally, shortly before the stores along Sunset Boulevard closed, I found a really raunchy old shop with a lot of beat-up masks and costumes in the window that had a large crack from top to bottom. The old gentleman who owned the place waited on me and said he'd had all kinds of requests but never one for a Hitler false face. He went to the back of the store, and for a full half hour he ducked in and out from behind a curtain, shaking his head and saying, "I'm looking, I'm looking." Then, suddenly, he appeared with a rubber mask of Hitler. He said he wanted a hundred dollars for it because Maximilian Schell had once worn it and signed it. It was a ridiculous price to pay, but I needed it and bought it.

A few nights passed. I was on my way to this big Halloween party in Beverly Hills. I knew I wouldn't be stopping anyplace along the way, so I suited up in my Hitler ensemble, pink uniform, mask and all. I was making my way across Fairfax, Hollywood's Jewish sector, in my black Mercedes-Benz when I had a blowout. Getting out of my car is the last thing I remember until I got where I am now, in the intensive care ward at Cedars Sinai Hospital. Apparently a large group of Jewish militants, who themselves had been beaten badly by a group of American Nazis, really did a number on me.

I guess next year, if there is a next year, I'll go back to the old reliable sheet with two eyes cut out. That always worked, even as a kid. But knowing my luck, I just might run into a nasty splinter group from the Ku Klux Klan.

THE SNOWMAN

Having to work in a city gets to you eventually. I don't care how sophisticated you think you are. There's something about growing up on a farm that never leaves you. It's hell while you're there, all those terrible chores, milking cows, shucking corn, slopping the pigs, digging fence posts, putting the rigs on the horses, stacking hay in the barn in August and on and on. For some unknown reason, you miss all that when you move away.

I've been away from the farm almost five years. So now, coming home for the holidays is especially fun. A chance to visit with Mom, taste her fabulous cooking, and to stroll around the farm with Dad. God, it was good to walk up the old gravel road to the main house and to feel the snow crunch under every step. It was cold, damn cold, but it felt good. Besides, I'd come prepared with a stocking cap, heavy wool jacket and sheepskin-lined boots. I stuck around the house through Christmas and then decided to call on a few old cronies from college days I thought might be home for a couple of weeks like myself.

I drove into town to just sort of look around and see if some of the old haunts were still standing. Only a couple were. The town looked like a Norman Rockwell painting. At its peak, during World War II, Sugar Creek, Vermont, had a huge population of 980. It was half that now.

Still, it had everything you'd want in a small town. There was the quaint little white Presbyterian church, Wally's Drugstore, Bick's Bait House, Emma's Diner, Lowell's Barber Shop and Sugar Creek Jail with never more than three occupants: Sheriff Lockstedder, his deputy, Buzz Smith, and the town drunk, Mitch (nobody ever knew his last name). It took all of an hour to see the old place. It dawned on me that if any of the old gang were home for the holidays, they'd be up at Rabbit Hill, where we all used to go sledding. When I arrived, sure enough, a dozen of them were there jumping on sleds. Funny somehow to see people in their mid-forties with mittens on, heavy sheepskin jackets, wool scarfs and heavy boots rolling around in that heavy powdered snow.

Of all people to be the first to greet me and offer me his sled was the town bully, Bear Jorgensen. He had put on a lot of weight and had quite a gut on him, but I'm sure he was still pretty tough. He threw those big arms around me and motioned to all the others to come on over. Then he pointed to a snowman, a really big snowman that stood at the base of the hill. Bear was always daring us to do something all through grade school, high school and even college, and here he was, a forty-five-year-old clown daring all of us forty-five-year-old clowns once more. So what do we do now, Bear? He motioned to the snowman. "Hit that rascal waist-high and I'll buy you a case of the best wine and a night on the town in your favorite joint in Boston," he said. "I'll even throw in my secretary, who's all of twenty-eight and will go anywhere as long as you've showered."

The snowman was probably the biggest one I'd ever seen. I couldn't understand why the kids hadn't put arms on him. I kept thinking, I've seen this snowman before, but where?

"Okay, Bear, you're on!" I finally answered. "Give us a shove, you old bastard!"

Away I went like a bat out of hell—I felt as if I were qualifying for the Olympics and the gold medal. I hit the snowman waist-high. Boy, did I ever. I think I'm still picking up the pieces of me *and* the sled. The snowman turned out to be a solid bronze statue of Admiral Byrd, the Antarctic explorer. Bear had set us up again!

Funny thing about little towns: buildings are torn down, people move away or die, or a major highway many times will cut right through; sometimes outsiders come through and scare the local people, but who would've thought the town bully would still be around.

AN OLD INDIAN
BURIES AN OLD FRIEND

When my friend was young, my, how he stood out in a room, whether in a city or out in the country. Everyone admired him so; I was so proud that he was my best friend.

How strong he was—an incredible body. And his eyes! At night, how far he could see like a great horned owl.

Suddenly he began to grow feeble—first his great eyes, and then his body. His old heart grew weaker and weaker; he would wheeze and then choke a great deal. But when you have a great and wonderful friend, you never abandon him.

When he started to go, it was as if everything in his great body was leaving him to travel with the Great Spirit on the other side.

I was the only one with him when he died. His great body gave one great shake—one huge cough—and then he was very still.

When I laid him to his rest, someone at the grave-side was playing a radio, or maybe it was his own. All I know is he was the best damn pickup truck I'd ever known.

THE POSTCARD

There is so much to tell you about this beautiful place. It's just the most breathtaking country I've ever seen. The architecture is unbelievably unique. The people are probably the sweetest and kindest (outside my family, of course) I've ever run into in all my travels. One cannot get enough of the artwork. I swear, every time you turn a corner, there's another painting. I can understand now why almost all the Impressionists came here for their holidays. The weather has been simply divine. I don't think I've seen more than a couple of clouds in the sky the whole time I've been here. They were big and fluffy.

Needless to say, the food is fantastic. Anything and everything is available. Would you believe there are seven different chefs, from seven different countries here at the inn? Having always gone first class does in the long run pay off. My rooms are small, but beautifully done in excellent taste, with all original antiques in *all* the rooms. Imagine, in my bedroom, the headboard belonged to Napoleon and Josephine when they were first married. The very desk I'm writing this postcard on belonged to Lord Nelson. It is said he wrote some of his last letters on this desk before sailing to Trafalgar.

It suddenly dawns on me that I'm writing you a letter and not a postcard at all. I suppose I shouldn't bring this up at this time, but I have purchased some fantastic antiques. The airfare cost me a bloody fortune, and from what I've already told you about the rooms I'm staying in, you can imagine what my bill will be like when I leave here. I've looked all over for some things I thought you might like, but unfortunately I've come up with nothing! I know you must find this hard to believe. . . .

Save this letter and stationery. It is some of the very stationery that Louis XIV used just before he abdicated his throne. With this letter, I'm including six glossy postcards from this lovely seaside resort. Oh, I know you don't smoke, but I'm bringing home an ashtray from this place, too. You can always put your paper clips, rubber bands and stamps in it. You'll come up with some use for it. Unfortunately, it isn't old! As a matter of fact, all the ashtrays in this sixteenth-century inn are made in Taiwan. So are the postcards, but the picture is authentic and, of course, so are the stamps. Hold on to these cards and stamps long enough and, I promise you, you won't be sorry.

It must be terrible to have been confined to your bed all these years, but I'm sure if you start pasting postcards around your room, it will be *almost* as good as if you were there in all those places. I'm sure you remember when postcards were a penny. Well, here they are, fifty cents apiece. I'll write tomorrow, if I can afford a card. . . .

MY HOMETOWN IS GONE—
I MEAN GONE

I hadn't been back in ten long years to my hometown, the little town of Bellbrook. The population, including livestock, some chickens and a dozen dogs and cats, was 412. But now, here I was driving across the country, pulling out of California toward Ohio, all by myself; that's the way I wanted it. I wanted, this time, to visit the town and the house I was born in, to take it all in as I did when I was a child and before I went away to World War II.

I was wondering if I'd see my old girlfriend Polly; I had a feeling, I don't know why, that she was married and hadn't moved away. And I got to thinking about the old creek, the Blue Hole, out on Mr. Weber's farm. It ran through the farm and had a lot of catfish and carp, and you could always count on some big largemouth bass toward the end of summer; someone who had written to me a few years back said the creek had dried up.

I felt that going back in the late spring was a really good time to be going home, as all the flowers and most of the trees—the dogwood, maple, wild cherry and buckeye—would be in bloom.

Of course, Mom and Dad wouldn't be there. Dad had come West years ago because of his asthma. Still, there'd be lots of cousins, old buddies and some gals to see. As I drove I kept thinking about how many of my old pals would still be alive. Well, here I was damn near sixty myself.

I had written ahead of time to the one good place to stay, the Whitemarsh Inn. As time went by and a few days passed, I finally found myself crossing the Indiana border into Ohio. My heart was skipping a few beats. I turned on the car radio and, wouldn't you know, it picked up some Glenn Miller music. Boy, did that remind me of those school dances at the top of the YMCA on Elm Street!

As I approached Bellbrook I saw about eight or ten state highway patrol cars, lights flashing, crisscrossing the main street. I got out of my car and asked one of the troopers what the problem was. He told me that about two hours ago a twister had hit the town and leveled it. The only building that managed to remain standing, he said, was the old First Presbyterian Church built about the time of the Civil War; surviving inside was the minister, about twenty-five old people and a few kids.

I turned my car around and headed west. As I saw the sign "You are now leaving the state of Ohio," I got to thinking that next Sunday I would definitely go back to church.

THE
MONEY PREACHER

They's a itty-bitty church us kids and Ma and Pa used to go to down near Possum Holler. It weren't very big—maybe fifty folks, and they was mostly middle-aged women and kids and a few old men— kinda like the whole bunch of them little churches all across them West Virginia mountains back in the fifties.

Ma made me and my brother go every Sunday no matter what the weather was like or even if we was sick and full o' fever, we had to go. The pastor, Mr. Lyle Stubbins, was a nice-lookin' man, and he had himself one heck of a good voice. Nobody went to sleep in *his* congregation. And if ya did, he said that if ya slept over two or three Sundays in a row, the Devil would eventually paralyze ya so's ya *never* could move again.

My brother Aaron was five year ahead of me. He liked the preacher and the preacher liked him. One summer before I moved away for good, Aaron went with Pastor Stubbins on what they called a retreat. They was gone for two whole weeks. When Aaron came back, he showed us a brand-new wristwatch, had him a pair of real good Sunday black shoes, a Bible with a gold cloth cover, and a 10K gold cross on a gold chain give to him by the program director of Station WSOL. And, for Pa and Ma, an eleven by fourteen of Jesus holdin' up the cross in one hand and the State of West Virginia in the other. Thing I liked about it was that it glowed in the night. Pastor Stubbins claimed my brother Aaron could heal people, and probably before another year were out, he'd be one of the biggest and bestest healers in the whole U.S.A.

Now, ever since we was younguns, Pa had asthma—funny now that Aaron had all these here powers he couldn't do nuthin' 'bout Pa. And Ma never walked right 'cause of her having a clubfoot. Aaron's answer to Ma and Pa was even though they was real good Christians, they still didn't have enough belief—elsewise they wouldn't be crippled up like they was.

It was bad for my brother that he couldn't heal Ma and Pa. It really bothered him. But he went on a-preachin' and a-healin'. He got so good at healin' he got his own TV show—a half hour—and he come into some real big money. He got him a brand-new car—cost as much as seventy-five thousand dollars. He got him two or three big homes—God knows what *they* come to! One day he was on his show and I was watchin' him. He had a man on who said he was a victim of real terrible migraines. Brother Aaron looked into the man's eyes, placed his hands on the man's head and commenced to shout out: "Jesus, oh sweet Jesus, cast the demons from this poor man's head!" The man looked into brother Aaron's eyes long and wildlike. And he hypnotized my brother and then whispered into his ear for at least a minute. All this on national television! My brother set there for a while and then stood up and confessed to everybody that he was a joke, that money had took over and totaled his mind. It was all the devil's doin', he said and then my brother screamed the worst: "I love the devil!"

When my brother Aaron come out of the trance, he run out of the studio and into the street. And from outa nowhere a bright red Mustang—a 1986 goin' full out, really burnin' rubber—smashed him and killed him dead. A hit-and-run. Nobody seen the driver and he was never caught. One little kid said he seen the license plate—they weren't no numbers, just letters that spelled out H-E-L-L.

THE BLACK LUNCH BOX

For years I walked to work. It was a long walk, a little over three miles, but it was always interesting. The many people—old, young, middle-aged; cats, dogs; even saw a big black snake once wiggle across some fresh cement. Sure, I could've taken the car or the bus, but I *wanted* to walk. Especially on those warm, sunny days, those beautiful days in the fall when the colors of the leaves were magnificent, and in spring with the birds singing, the buds on the trees coming out and the flowers just beginning to show.

My old black lunch box was my friend, and I'd swing it alongside of me as I crossed one street after another. I always left early in the morning, so I'd usually see kids waiting for the bus to pick them up. Of course the milkman couldn't figure out why I walked. And neither could the newspaper boy, throwing the daily news up on the house porches. From time to time dogs, big and little, would run out to bark at me, but most of the time they'd just jump up and I'd transfer my lunch box to my other hand and give them a pat.

Over the years the neighborhood hadn't changed much. You'd see the occasional beat-up pickup truck parked in a driveway, or a wild, shiny motorcycle leaning against the side of a badly painted duplex, a broken skateboard, and now and then some kids would throw an empty six-pack of beer bottles on the lawn of a wealthy family who had an iron jockey in front of their home. But things were fine, generally, you couldn't ask for a nicer place to be.

The last day I walked to work I saw something that frightened me. Suddenly, at least a dozen or more homes had all kinds of graffiti on them, with some really raunchy sayings sprayed on the stucco. The newspaper boy no longer rode his bike; his dad was driving him. I noticed the kid was having trouble throwing the paper—he was wearing a cast on his arm because he'd been mugged. I also realized there weren't nearly as many youngsters waiting for the old yellow bus. And when they did wait at the corner, they were accompanied by their parents; six children had been molested the day before. Then I saw a large police dog lying dead on a lawn—it had been poisoned. The milkman had canceled his run; seems he'd been shot, and now he's in the hospital, not expected to live.

This would be the last day I'd ever walk to work. The neighborhood hadn't just changed. It was, for all intents and purposes, gone. I was nervous. And within a block of the factory a car pulled up to the curb and a man with a ski mask motioned me over—he had a .45 in his hand.

"*Get in, now*, or I'll blow you away!" he said. "Do you hear me, *now!*"

I thought I'd drop dead, right then and there. But I got in.

The man at the wheel jerked off his ski mask, threw the gun in the backseat, laughed uproariously and said, "Joe—*April Fool*! You clown! Don't you recognize me?" It was my boss! Big joke, huh? But it was the last day I walked to work.

THE
CARDBOARD MAN

As far as one could see there were the bodies of men—a few young men, a number of middle-aged men and a number of old men. Most of these derelicts were lying on strips of cardboard with their feet and hands wrapped in newspapers. These men are found not only in cities in America but in large metropolitan areas all over the world. What used to be called "bums" are now labeled "misfits, unfortunates, mental cases, alcoholics and drug addicts."

The cardboard man I saw was leaning against a building whose walls were covered with all kinds of graffiti. His hair was filthy and gave the appearance at first glance of having had car wax smeared on it. His eyes were badly swollen and completely bloodshot. His face was a mass of sores, and the only areas not raw and open were covered by his beard. Looking at his throat, one could see an old scar that ran from his Aadm's apple to his left ear. Someone had tried to kill him—whether during the day or night is anybody's guess. These men all seemed to seek one another out and ended up always in the heart of the city not too far from the Midnight Mission.

How had the cardboard man come to be here? Now he was preparing his so-called bed for the evening. He had no more than half a dozen squares of cardboard, all in separate pieces, which he would sleep on. As he lay stretched out I saw what appeared to be dog tags that had fallen out over a blackened T-shirt. And then I saw that all the fingers on both of his hands were covered with rings. And I might add they all looked very real.

The man next to me gave me a big jab in the ribs and said, "Whatever you do, don't try to take any of those rings off the cardboard man, he'll kill you. It's all a setup. He used to be a professional soldier—a mercenary—and he baits these poor devils. You'll never believe what *he* collects—no, it ain't rings! He collects *fingers!*"

THE
FISHERMAN

Old Jake McAllister was by far the best fisherman in these parts. I mean that old man fished hard all day, and sometimes all night. He's still got the biggest largemouth bass ever to come out of a river, lake or pond in all of Clark County. It's still hangin' down there at Weber Sporting Goods Store on East Main. Stuffed, it weighed out at twelve and a half pounds. Why, ain't a bass ever come close to bein' took that size since before World War II!

Old Jake is eighty-five now and still fishin'. Ain't nobody really knows where his "spots" are. He ain't never told nobody, 'ceptin' me, and I sure would never

give him away. He let me in on a couple of places like
Wolf Creek and Big Muddy, but he never would let
me go with him personal.

I been over to his place well over a dozen times
durin' fishing season. He lived in a old barn he done
over into a house about twenty miles outa town. He
raised vegetables, had a coupla goats, sheep, chickens,
and a old yeller dog called Goober. Jake also had him
a big deep freeze, where he kept all his extra fish.
And I want to tell ya he had him a lot of fish in that
big old white box, maybe a coupla hundred pounds.

One night when I was about fourteen, jes' before
the fishin' season started to let up, I was over to his
house. Him and me was havin' some real good eats
(ain't nobody could cook fish like old Jake could). He
started in tellin' some fish stories after we done the
dishes. Course, a lot of them stories was about "them
rascals that got away!" He told me how he was writ
up in some real important magazines like *Outdoor
Life* and *Sports Afield*. And 'cause he was an old
country boy, he even made his own fly rods, tied his
own flies, even designed himself a spin-casting reel.
He came in second in casting in the state, and eleventh
in the nation—and he did all this when he turned
sixty. Jake told me he'da been *first* in the country, but

he had to work hard most of his life and didn't get to really fish till he was into his fifties. Them rich guys, he would say, "got it made, they jes' sit on their ass, set the hook when they get a hit and reel in. Everythin' else is did fer 'em!"

I looked over at old Jake jes' before the fire in the fireplace was about to go out and asked him his best piece of advice he could give me, as I had a lot of fishin' days ahead of me. "Kid," he said, "sportsmen come and go, they use all kinds of fancy rods and lines, hooks and lures. You want to eat good when you come home at night? Wanna fill that stringer? Get ya stick of dynamite, throw it in the lake, and yer gonna fill yer white box jes' as full as mine is. A lota people would say Old Jake's a lousy sportsman and that they should take his awards away from him, even take that big largemouth bass down that's hangin' in Weber's. But all I can say is everybody wears a couple of hats, they's a good and a bad side to us all. Hell, look at all them politicians up there in Washington— they always tell the truth till they get elected, then they commence to lie a lot."

All I know is, old Jake didn't *have* to tell me about any of his favorite spots, but he did, and I *still* do real good and he was one hell of a man at cookin' fish.

Oh, I might add Old Jake is gone now some fifteen years. Big muddy has been rerouted, diverted, whatever, Wolf Creek is contaminated and about dried up and all over the state construction crews is dynamitin' everythin', puttin' up houses.

LOST VALLEY OF
THE GODS

When I was a little boy, my brother and I used to stretch out on the big thick Indian rug in our den and unfold a map of the United States. We'd run our fingers across it, stop at a certain spot and pretend that we were famous explorers and had discovered the state our fingers landed on.

We were always fascinated by treasure hunts, finding gold and silver, and as time went on we both went off to visit old mine shafts, rivers that supposedly had gold veins and other such places. Almost every spring we would head out with our backpacks, picks, shovels, cooking gear, maps, canteens, etc., always with the hope of hitting it big.

It was on one of these treks that we found ourselves in Indian country, just on the edge of the Shoshone Reservation in the northwest corner of Wyoming. An old Shoshone chief known as Two Bears sold us a map for five hundred dollars; he claimed it would lead us to a great treasure in a place called Lost Valley situated at the very end of the Teton Mountains.

The old chief, Two Bears, said he once saw the treasure with his own eyes. His dad had been a miner who on his days off would search for malachite, the beautiful green semiprecious stone found only in Wyoming and in parts of Russia. It was when Two Bears and his dad were hauling chunks of malachite back to their pack mules that an entire side of a mountain caved in. When the dust cleared, they found themselves standing in the Lost Valley of the Gods. The way the sun's rays hit the mountain's sides made it look like one solid sheath of gold.

We listened to Two Bears' tale, took the map, and set out to be millionaires. We didn't take any of it too seriously, but after almost three weeks of looking for the Lost Valley, we actually found it. The old Indian's map had led us to the exact place. We set up camp, and looking around, we knew we were in for a lot of hard work, sore backs, blistered hands, long days and even longer nights; we sweated all that spring, through the summer and into the fall. Then, incredibly, in the third week in September, we found the treasure. We had to dynamite, which neither of us like to do, because we looked upon it as hurting the mountain. But we did it anyway, and after the explosion we realized that we had (just guessing, of course) well over a couple of million dollars in gold.

We packed up all we could, and after two weeks of rough going, coming down from the mountain, we finally arrived in the little village of Elk River, a spot where the painter Frederic Remington had once summered. Almost immediately, we went to the assay office to weigh in our fortune. And while my brother and I were there a man came in with a newspaper that said, "The Treasury Department has declared that gold is no longer a precious metal. It is henceforth worth nothing."

My brother and I looked at each other and almost simultaneously roared in laughter.

A few days later, as we were leaving Elk River, we noticed a little museum. For some reason, we decided to go in. As we were talking to the curator, my brother dropped Two Bears' "gold map" on the floor. The curator picked it up, placed it on one of the glass tables and unrolled it.

"Gentlemen, do you have any idea of what you have here?" he said. "I could be wrong, but I would bet my wife and two sons that this is a hand-painted map done by Frederic Remington. Here, you can see for yourselves—it's even dated. If I were you, I'd send this on to Washington just to be sure."

He told us that if this map of Remington's was authentic, it would be worth at least $1 million. Not long after, my brother and I went to Washington and to New York; we found out the map *was* authentic and we received $1.2 million. We gave Two Bears two hundred thousand, kept the million and started collecting old maps.

Now we are quite old; we never married, but keep a wonderful home not far from the Shoshone Reservation. And if ever you were to visit us, you'd find two white-haired brothers stretched out on an old Indian rug running their fingers across old maps.

THE
MARATHON RUNNER

Throughout the year marathons take place all over the world. And, of course, a number of them are held here in the United States. Most of the runners, whether they're men or women, are comparatively young, have been running most of their lives, and above all are in good condition—very good condition. The contestants in these races come from all sections of the world.

The marathon I decided to enter was a big and famous one—the Boston Marathon. Back on the reservation in Montana I had been an athlete—good in football and baseball and outstanding in track. I won the state finals, and had my mother and dad not been killed in a car crash in my freshman year in college, I really believe I might've had a crack at the Olympics. My dad had left my three sisters and myself a 1,500-acre ranch on the Blackfoot Reservation where we raised mainly cattle. My Indian name is Joe Little Turtle.

I shall always remember my grandfather, one of the tallest Indians I'd ever seen, saying, "Remember, Joe. Behold the turtle! The only time he makes progress is when he sticks his neck out." He lived to be a hundred and three and got up one day in early March of 1970, threw his corncob pipe in the fireplace and said, "I shook hands with Teddy Roosevelt and accompanied him on a worldwide tour, corresponded with Will Rogers and was present when Apollo Eleven, with Neil Armstrong aboard, took off for the moon. I've seen enough, enough for me." Grandfather grabbed a hand shovel from a corner of the room and said, "I'm going out to dig a grave—don't nobody follow till two suns pass. Then if them turkey buzzards and coyotes ain't got to me, throw some lime on me, say what ya want and be on about your business!"

When I won the state finals in high school in Great Falls, Montana, I was wearing my grandfather's moccasins. At first they were going to disqualify me for not wearing the right gear, but then the officials got together and overruled the decision.

I had to spend most of my time working on the ranch tending to the cattle. Meat was not selling well and my sisters were all going to college, so I shelved my running dreams, but I did find myself running as much as I could on the ranch, whenever I could find the time. This was especially true during the winter months when it was bitterly cold, and I mean *cold*, as much as forty below this past winter. The heavy snow and high drifts would always strengthen my legs. Come spring and the thaw I found I could run like a deer.

When I turned sixty, I decided that before I packed it in I would go to Boston, hoping that I would pass all the requirements so I could at least enter the race.

I must confess I never dreamed of winning it. There were too many finer athletes, so much younger than myself. All I wanted to do, like many people my age, was to make a good showing and just finish. I notified my sisters that I was on my way back East to Boston to enter the marathon. Three of them were married and living not on the reservation but in others parts of the country. The night before I left Montana all the men of my tribe had a big council meeting to which I brought my grandfather's peace pipe. Originally the pipe had four eagle feathers attached to it; now there was only one. Also the bowl on the pipe had a large crack in it. There were eleven of us and we all puffed on the pipe. It was strange, I could feel my grandfather's presence—as a matter of fact, before the smoke cleared, it had formed the shape of a turtle. "Behold the turtle—the only time he makes progress is when he sticks his neck out!"

The next day I drove down to Great Falls, boarded the plane and was on my way to Boston. The day of the race I did something I had wanted to do ever since I was a small boy. I wanted to run just wearing a pair of buckskins, a beaded band around my head and a pair of moccasins. I had painted a turtle on my chest. I was the only full-blooded American Indian in the whole darn marathon. Joe Little Turtle, Blackfoot, age sixty from Rocky Boy, Montana. I could describe the whole race, but I won't take the chance of boring you.

Just *when* I came across the finish line I don't remember. I *do* remember my sisters were there and all the tribal chiefs. I won—I crawled across the finish line as my heart was giving out. Just before my eyes closed forever, I saw my grandfather. I felt a sharp pain in my right hand and looked at it. There was a picture of a turtle, and he was smiling.

THE
CAMPERS

Every spring, for as long as I can remember, our family would camp out on Prospector's Point somewhere at the base of the Rockies. I say "somewhere" because Grandfather first found it when he came to California with thousands of others during the Gold Rush in 1849; he never did strike it rich, but he loved the country, sent for Grandmother and they settled in. Grandfather would never tell outsiders about Prospector's Point, and even today it remains a secret place and to my knowledge only our family knows its whereabouts. I guess you could spot it from the air because it's almost a perfect circle maybe fifty feet across and very flat—the top of a mountain. It's so high, so remote, it always took a full day to get to it.

This spring we decided that just my wife and I and two of our oldest friends, Betty and Jim would camp out for all of Easter week. Needless to say, if you've never climbed before, it's tough and can be scary. Not only is it tough on the old body, but carrying gear makes it even rougher. The day we ascended, things were just as tough as we'd anticipated, but it was also very cold. Just before darkness we finally threw our gear down on the dusty flat surface of Prospector's Point. What an incredible view, clear as far as you could see! And directly above us, no more than a couple of hundred feet, was a magnificent bald eagle, circling. In unison we laughed as we gave the old astronaut yell "The Eagle has landed!"

Even though we were tired, we quickly set up camp. We got the tents up, rolled out the sleeping bags, devoured a couple of sandwiches each and settled in for the night. All was peaceful. The main concern on top of a mountain, miles from nowhere, is that everyone get along if you're staying for a week— especially because things can get very close up there. But we all loved to read (some of us even considered ourselves writers), the four of us were good friends and had a lot in common—Betty was a damn good photographer, and I'm an old-fashioned bird watcher —so we had a lot to look forward to in sharing our mutual interests.

The week passed like a dream. Until the last night. There was no wind, so we decided it would be all right to build a small fire. We were sitting around it when one of the largest bears I'd ever seen jumped into the center of us, waving his massive arms and growling, almost screeching. With one fell swoop he knocked the two women off the mountaintop, and quickly swung around and drove a mountaineer's pick through Jim's chest. I remembered the .38 special I had hanging on the tent pole, grabbed it, pointed it right at the bear's face and fired. He staggered for a minute, then fell back, falling just short of the rim of the mountaintop. It had all lasted maybe thirty seconds.

I looked around and saw I was the only one alive. I ran to each victim—both women had broken necks and Jim had been killed instantly. Somehow, in the commotion, I had badly broken my ankle and a part of the bone in my lower right foot was sticking out an inch or two. All I could do now was wait—for somebody down below to find us or, hopefully, a chopper to pass overhead. I kept thinking how lucky I was that although Prospector's Point was a secret, it could still be seen from the air.

I must've been up there for at least two days, maybe three, when a helicopter finally did spot me and the others. I'd kept a fire going and a ranger had seen the smoke. Since it was a small chopper, it wasn't too difficult for him to set it down. Though I knew that the helicopter was overweight, I insisted that we had to get my wife's and our friends' bodies off that mountaintop. The pilot took a chance but he managed to get them on board. As he started up the big rotor blade, I suddenly saw my Nikon camera dangling from a nail on the tent pole where the revolver had been. I pleaded with the pilot to grab it. I needed it for a lot of reasons. A lot of words were exchanged, but he got out and retrieved it for me.

Several weeks later as I was recuperating at home the local camera shop sent back the pictures I had taken on Prospector's Point. I knew how valuable these pictures would be because they were the last pictures taken of my wife and my friends. I would never see them again.

All the pictures were in color and came out clear as a bell; there was great tranquillity in all our faces. And then I came across a picture of the bear. It showed him from his head to his waist; I suppose the shutter must have gone off accidentally when I reached for my gun. The incredible thing about the photo was that the bear had the face of a man. Granted it was covered with fur, but when have you seen a grizzly bear with blue eyes?

Nothing could be proven—by me, the rangers or the other investigating teams. Even the local coroner said that when he examined the bear's body, the eyes were brown. But in my picture they were blue. Also, when you looked closely at the bear's right ear, you could see a tiny golden earring. The police explained that many bears, when they are cubs, are found by campers and tagged with unusual objects.

ANIMAL
TALES

THE
VISITOR

I went to see a friend of mine today to visit for a little while. We had been pals for almost eighteen years and were together almost constantly. He paid more attention to me than even my own mom and dad. He almost never spoke, but when he did, it was short, sweet and, I might add, loud. It was his eyes, big brown melting eyes, that said everything. He was my dog, Growler.

I remember the day he died, because I was the one who found him. Mom and Dad were on vacation in the Northeast. I can't recall how long I stood looking down at him, hoping against hope that he was only kidding and playing dead. I hoped he would jump up and go after that big old yellow rubber bone.

He didn't jump up. He was dead, all right. His old heart had finally given out. He didn't have to go down the road to get the newspaper anymore.

I carried him to an old elm tree he used to lie under, and there I buried him. I was the only one at his burial, except for a big fox squirrel who stood there for a long while before scampering up the tree. I made a little cross out of an old orange crate for his marker. Then I knelt down and said some words— words right from my heart.

I looked around for Spots, the old cat Growler had loved to chase. Nowhere to be seen. My thoughts then turned to Goldie, a beautiful female golden Labrador. She and Growler had been great pals. I'm sure Goldie must have been off chasing rabbits or something. I had almost forgotten—there was also a wild cottontail that had become very tame and would come right up to old Growler's nose.

As I stood up I turned around and saw the cotton-tail standing on his hind legs adjacent to the cross I'd made. So old Growler did have a mourner after all.

The rabbit paid his respects and, typically, hopped across the fresh sod I had just put down.

I thought of the funerals I'd been to, the cemeteries, and how not many people left their footprints on a new grave.

THANKSGIVING

wonder if you realize what we go through? It's not that far removed from guys who are doing time. A few years go by while you're confined to a small area with a lot of chicken wire around you. Some farmer throws some feed to you, you get a little water and all you do is walk around in the compound waiting, waiting for the end of November.

Later, some guy, a rancher or a farmer, arrives and you know it's all over. You thought the days of the guillotine had ended? Forget it! I've seen a sister's or brother's head placed on the stump, a man with a good-sized ax lop it off in one fell swoop. Next thing you know, the bodies are plucked, washed and sealed into some plastic bags and they're off to the supermarkets.

People give a blessing over us, a series of things to be thankful for in the past year and thanks for what they hope will be a better year coming up. Funny, they just say some prayers only that once, on Thanksgiving. But we pray every day, sometimes all day, from the time we're born until the moment we hit the chopping block. We really live a day at a time.

People will tell one another, regardless of what time of year it is or what occasion, that everything happens for the best. If that's true, I have to think the only things we feel fairly good about are the turkey dinners that are served to the poor people or the guys down at the missions.

You're not going to believe this, but if there is reincarnation, you know what I want to come back as? A blind farmer with a rubber ax. Either that, or be able to know exactly when November comes around so I can fly to some distant primitive island where they worship us.

If you're getting ready to say your prayers at the dinner table—and I'm sure you have a lot to be thankful for—do us a favor and say one for us.

THE LAST DAY
THE CIRCUS CAME
TO TOWN

When I was a little boy a long time ago, one of the things all of us kids looked forward to was the circus coming to town. "The Greatest Show on Earth," as it was billed by Ringling Brothers and Barnum & Bailey. Getting up at four o'clock in the morning didn't bother us at all. After all, that was when we could see the most exciting part of the circus —the unloading. The elephants were moving the cages, and big tough men were handling all kinds of rigs and gear. There were pretty ladies everywhere, and the clowns ran around while jugglers did last-minute practicing. A man would be feeding the tigers as the calliope cranked up to tell the towns-people to "wake up, the circus is coming."

On one particular hot August day way back in 1935 all the kids were watching the circus train pull into town. How beautiful the train was with all its cars and their colorful decorations! It was just about to come to a stop when I saw a switchman, a railroad switchman, scurry across the tracks. He was too late.

A fast freight hit the circus train head-on. That freight must have been doing at least eighty-five miles per hour. I'll never forget the sound.

Every one of those circus cars went every which way. Not one of them stayed on the tracks. There were screams. Lions, tigers and elephants roamed. There were cries from a bunch of dwarfs huddled next to a dead camel.

It seemed as if all the cages had broken open and all the animals were running everywhere. People were yelling, running, stumbling and falling over one another to get out of the way. The police, all six of them, were firing guns in the air. One big elephant had to be shot; the former commander of Post 37 of the American Legion, using a Thompson submachine gun, blew him away. Big Boy Jumbo was all over Main Street.

My sister and I were running down Elmwood

Avenue when we spotted a Bengal tiger in the bushes. A black circus worker had cold-cocked him, hitting him with his fist; the tiger was out like a light. We dragged that big rascal into our home and, believe it or not, he remained tame, behaving like a big pussy cat.

Although the circus doesn't come to town anymore, once a year my sister and I dress up as clowns, put Stripes on a leash, and walk down Main Street on August 4, the day the circus used to come to town.

MY BIRD DOESN'T SING ANYMORE

My bird is beautiful. He's the most beautiful little bird I've ever seen. Some years ago my grandmother gave me a lovely cage for him. When I first got him, oh, how he sang! You could hear him from the kitchen to the front door. I cleaned him ever so carefully. He and his cage always looked immaculate. He was on our mantelpiece, right in the middle, where everyone who came into our living room could see him.

I was the only one who could get him to sing. I showed him more attention than anybody else, so it was only natural he would sing for *me*! He is a small bird, about the size of a bluebird and enhanced with almost every color in the rainbow. He's truly one of a kind. I wonder why he won't sing anymore? I can't for the life of me think what I might have done to cause him to be miffed at me. Maybe I forgot to wind him up.

DID ANYONE
SEE MY DOGGIE?

Did anyone see my doggie? He ran away from home, I think, or maybe he was stolen. I don't think he was sick. He barked this morning when I fed him and he barked again and ran out to the gate before I left for school.

His name is Scratchy.

He's snaggy, medium-sized, kinda old and has a slight limp. Please call if you see him; please bring him back.

I have a reward. It's only fifteen dollars, but it's all I have.

He's housebroken—if you do decide to keep him.

Please don't let him stay outside all night. He'll only bark. That's 'cause his paw hurts him when it gets real cold.

I've had him ever since he was a puppy. My granddad gave him to me years ago. He's really part of the family. I need him badly.

He's never bitten anybody, chased a cat or tinkled on Mom's flowers. I wish I was older so I could drive Dad's pickup and drive around until I found him.

I don't know where to begin to look for Scratchy. I know we should never have left the farm and come to this big old city. I don't blame Scratchy if he *did* decide to run away. Nobody likes the city. I'll bet anything it was a nail or glass, maybe even a gun that made Scratchy limp 'cause he never had that limp while we were livin' on the farm.

Oh, by the way—Scratchy can sit up for you if you hold a dog biscuit. At least he does for me. He can even bring in the newspaper—not always, you understand, but most of the time.

Maybe I've told you too much about him and you'll decide to keep him for your own.

I wish he could talk. I bet if he could, he could really tell you a lot of things. He's almost sixteen years old, and that's real old for a dog. I'll bet you anything, the first thing he'd tell you is how he came to hurt his paw. We don't have any other pets and I miss him so much.

Dad says he ate too much anyway. Mom says his bark the last couple of years was weak and he was no good at being a watchdog anymore.

Funny, they sure looked hard for Grandpa when he got lost. Course, he was always down at Blue Moon Pool Hall, or at the Elks, and one thing for sure, he didn't bark at all!

Oh Scratchy, come on home! I'll work extra hard so I can get you some real good bones from Mr. Weber at the meat market. You're in my prayers every night. You always have been. I know God is watching over you. I never told you this, Scratchy—as if it would make any difference to you—but I made a special trip to Saint Thomas' Catholic Church. In the back they have a big statue of Saint Francis, you know, the patron saint of all the animals. I left what change I had at his feet. I don't think you can buy his love, but if anybody can help me find you, it's him. I sure hope he don't mind my being a Presbyterian.

ODE TO
A BABY ROBIN

Spring takes on a different perspective when you're high up in a maple tree. Everything looks incredibly beautiful, even the wildflowers. But to be born all fuzzy with huge bulblike eyes, frail wings and huge feet is kind of a sad start, a frightening beginning. Then to have to say good-bye to your brother and two sisters, Mom and Dad and get a good hold on the lip of the nest and *fly*! Knowing your wings are pathetically small compared with your head and body makes you wonder whether it's worth it to grow up; sticking your beak in the ground to pull out worms doesn't sound too exciting, anyway. Besides, a lot of babies never live to see one month, let alone a year. Why? Cats. Cats seem to know the exact day a baby is born and they lie waiting, fifteen or twenty feet from the tree. You would think Friskies would be enough for those clowns.

I was told by Dad that tomorrow I would fly and that I was long overdue. Everybody else had left the nest over a week ago. I told him I was afraid, mostly because I was the smallest of the four of us. My dad came right back and said, "Look, your two sisters and your brother made it, so can you!" I prayed that maybe that cat would go away, maybe he would get sick or a dog could come along and tree him.

What are my odds of surviving? Sure, my brother and two sisters made it, but they were bigger. I'm the runt. I wonder if there is a species of birds that doesn't have to fly, but just sits in a tree, eats the bugs in the dead limbs, munches on some berries or whatever. It's like some people who are born in an apartment, grow up, grow old and die there. I thought surely Mom would side with me and stall Dad someway, somehow. But no, she said she wouldn't stand having a "mama's boy" in the nest; what would the neighbors think?

The night before I was to fly, I had a long talk with Dad about life in general. "If I make it," I asked Dad, "and I fly and I survive, what would be my reward?"

He thought for a while but all he could come up with was, "Every ornithologist knows that the first sign of spring is seeing a robin redbreast—and maybe you'll be that robin." It didn't seem like a great reward to me.

And so the day came when I was to fly. My God! Looking down at the ground petrified me, but the most terrifying thing was that cat lying down there just twenty feet from the tree.

Dad and Mom gave me a half a garden worm, wished me luck and pushed me out. Boy, I was falling fast! From out of nowhere, a huge great horned owl grabbed me just before I hit the ground. (I'll never forget the expression on the cat's face, it was the ultimate "aw, shit" look.) Mr. Owl took me to a huge pine tree where he lived. I was sure that I was going to be his dessert, but I was fooled. He told me that as a robin I may be a songbird, but intelligence-wise I wasn't far removed from a sparrow. He said he would raise me to be the brightest robin anywhere in the continental United States. He also assured me that he would scare the crap out of any cat that bothered me.

I thought of Mom and Dad and my brother and sisters, but I couldn't pass up this opportunity. It would have been like picking night school at Whittier over MIT. And, after all, Mr. Owl also promised he'd teach me how to fly! As high as the Space Shuttle, he said.

Right now, though, Mr. Owl is gone, and would you believe it, there's another cat at the base of the tree. Maybe I ought to wait around for an eagle to grab me.

ODE TO
A SEA GULL

You know, being a sea gull isn't as bad as you might think. At least, it's not bad being an East or West Coast sea gull. Now, lake gulls are a bore. They're always saying, "We're just a step away from being buzzards because we're scavengers!"

But sea gulls get all kinds of goodies. Naturally, we get parts of fish, because a lot of us are always hanging around piers and docks. You might be surprised, though, to hear that I've also had a couple of sips of a Diet Pepsi, some domestic caviar, a big piece of a submarine sandwich, a lollipop, potato chips (which are okay) and crackers, though only when there is nothing else. Once, I even swallowed a 1925 dime. I never could pass the damn thing. Come to think of it, I've never since been able to take off or land the way I used to.

Being an Eastern gull has its good points, especially in Maine. A Maine gull lands on those lobster baskets and pots and those red and white buoys, watching all the fishermen coming in with their catch and then heading out again. A man in a yellow slicker looks neat, especially if he has a beard and a carved pipe. He's like us, our colors are kind of neat, too—at least, I think so. They're white, light gray with a big yellow beak. When it comes to looks, the only birds who give us competition on the beach are pelicans and sandpipers. Still, we all seem to get along remarkably well.

I spend a lot of time thinking. About a lot of different things. Like what happened to my cousin. Some fishermen were fishing and throwing a lot of bait in the water. A whole bunch of gulls were swooping down over the waves making passes at the bait. My cousin got a hook caught in his mouth and he's been benched ever since.

Being a West Coast gull, wow! Do they ever have it good, especially on those Southern California beaches, gliding over all those would-be starlets. The marinas seem to be prettier, especially around New-port and San Diego. Then there's Pebble Beach, Mon-terey and San Francisco. I'd like to fly all the way to the top of the Golden Gate and take a nice big jump hoping I'd hit the deck of a huge white cruise ship as she passes under the bridge on her way to the Orient.

Flying in the fog is a drag. You think it's bad for pilots? It's just as bad for us. Remember, we're not owls; our radar isn't nearly as good as theirs or those guys that fly the planes.

What can I tell you about our nesting habits? I came into this world on the top of a badly faded yel-low Mexican bus. The bus broke down just this side of the Napa Valley along the Pacific Coast Highway. The people in the bus abandoned it and left it to rot. Mom and Dad figured this was as good a time as any to have a baby. I was born in a crate of shriveled lemons. Dad flew immediately into a vineyard and really got bombed! Mom and Dad talked about that for years.

You know, I just happened to think of something—I wonder if any other gull ever thought about this. I'd really hate to be a kite. It's not so much being paper, it's just knowing that no matter how high that kid lets you fly and twist and turn in the blue sky, sooner or later he's going to reel you in and your freedom is gone. Oh, one other thing: I do hope that someday in a pirate movie, one of us will be on a pirate's shoulder instead of a parrot.

THE LITTLE BEAR
WHO DIDN'T KNOW WHO
HE WAS

Once upon a time, deep in a big green forest, lived a beautiful little brown bear named Grizzie. He was named after his great-grandfather, who died a few years ago after swallowing a jar in a trailer camp outside Yellowstone National Park.

Grizzie, who was all of ten years old, was told by his parents, a great horned owl (who was a part-time doctor) and an eagle (who was also a doctor) that he would never grow up to be a full-sized bear. Needless to say, all of his friends—Frank Fox, Ralph "Snowshoe" Rabbit, Sam "Little Red" Squirrel, Bill "Bad

Boy" Badger and a wild horse called "Stud"—began
to turn their backs on him. They would no longer
engage him in conversation or ever throw a glance his
way.

Little by little, Grizzie developed an inferiority
complex and isolated himself deeper and deeper in a
cave in the great green forest. Why, he asked himself,
have they done this to me? Why have they turned
their backs on me? Is it because I've stopped growing?
Am I a freak? What is it?

One night during a full moon, Dr. Oliver Owl, a
friend of the family and a former friend of Grizzie's,
flew into the cave where Grizzie was hiding.

"Dr. Owl," Grizzie cried out as the owl hovered
near the mouth of the cave, "please speak to me, give
me a minute of your time. Please, I beg you. I can't
go on much longer. What is it about me that no one
will speak to me?"

Dr. Owl opened his eyes, both of them as large as
two silver dollars, and ruffled his wings. "The creatures of the forest have always loved you," Dr. Owl
said. "Your problem with your growth means nothing. What *does* bother them is that your eyes have
somehow become buttons, your tongue is a red piece
of cloth, and you've been wearing a red bandanna

around your neck. They think you've turned into a store-bought teddy bear, and that someone has put a hex and evil curse on you!"

Grizzie thought for a moment and asked if Dr. Owl would take him to the Our Lady of the Unusual orphanage to be placed there in a child's arms. Dr. Owl agreed. He scooped up Grizzie and they flew to the orphanage.

Sure enough, a window was open and Dr. Owl flew in and placed Grizzie in a bed alongside a rosy-cheeked little boy. Dr. Owl said good-bye to Grizzie, told him he would tell the creatures of the forest where he was now and that he would visit him from time to time, especially during a full moon.

No sooner had Dr. Owl flown out the window than Grizzie looked over at the little boy whose head was resting on the pillow, the little boy with button eyes and a Velcro tongue.

THE
EASTER BUNNY

The Easter bunny is loved almost as much as Santa Claus. While Santa brings lots of toys for boys and girls to open on Christmas Day and, as a little bonus, fills all the stockings on Christmas Eve, Mr. Bunny only delivers Easter eggs.

But you'll have to admit they're always beautifully colored, well hidden, and each little boy and girl gets to hunt them and usually finds a chocolate bunny and lots of jelly beans.

The Easter bunny has to deliver eggs all over the United States and a few other countries. Because of this task, he has a very sore elbow and must get a lot of cortisone shots in his arm the following day. And since he has to hop everywhere, the tremendous pressure has affected his spine; he's really in constant pain, but he hides it very well. He always—well, almost always—wears a smile. Needless to say, the night before he hides all the Easter eggs, he has to swallow all sorts of different liquid colors and then decorate the hard-boiled eggs by sitting ever so carefully on each one.

Mr. Bunny loves you boys and girls, and although he's living with a lot of stress, he says, "It's all worth it, I wouldn't have it any other way. Besides, it's my only opportunity to go to Washington and hide eggs on the president's lawn." As Mr. Bunny is ever so fond of the poor, he always hides a number of eggs near the picket fence that runs around the White House so that the local kids can reach in and get them. Oh, one last thing, boys and girls: no matter what anybody tells you, Mr. Bunny can lay eggs—but only on Easter Sunday.

THE BIRD
THAT COULDN'T FLY

Along time ago, in the land of make-believe, lived a bird known to all the birds around him as Chirp. Chirp was a pretty little bird with yellow, black, light green and blue tail feathers. He was not large, not small, but just an average-size bird. He was on the songbird list and he got his name because he could warble a number of melodious tunes. How well Chirp sang! Without a doubt, he was the singingest bird in the forest.

But poor Chirp couldn't fly. He tried and tried for weeks, months and years. He went to all kinds of birds, big and little, to find out how he could fly.

Nobody could help him. Chirp's little feet were always so sore because he had to walk every place, but he still sang and chirped everywhere he went.

One day the great red-tailed hawk said to Chirp, "You know, I'm the largest bird in this forest and I can fly higher than all the birds. But you know something? I can't sing at all." So Chirp came to the conclusion that it wasn't so bad that he was the only bird in the forest that couldn't fly. Soon he also discovered that many of his feathered friends (and some other animals) wanted to chirp the way he did. So Chirp began to teach. Before long all the birds in the forest could sing at least one of Chirp's songs.

Not long after, there came to the forest a tall middle-aged man known to the birds and animals as the Tall Person. He was at least six feet six inches, and he would wander into the woods in the spring, summer, fall and winter. He always brought with him a sleeping bag, a knapsack full of food, binoculars and a tape recorder. He loved to record the sounds of the birds, and most of all, he loved to record Chirp.

The Tall Person and Chirp soon became good friends. Chirp became so friendly with him that he would jump on the Tall Person's shoulder, eat out of the palm of his hand and walk with him through the forest. One beautiful spring day, Chirp saw the Tall

Person sitting on an old stump. Chirp walked over to him and hopped on his shoulder. The Tall Person put his hand over his lips and told Chirp to put his feathers over his beak and be very still and listen. The Tall Man then turned on his tape recorder, which began to play back all of Chirp's songs one after another for a full hour. He then showed Chirp an album jacket with a full-color picture of Chirp on the cover.

He was whispering something in Chirp's ear when suddenly there was a whirring sound. In a nearby clearing in the forest a great helicopter, shaped and painted like a bird, landed. The Tall Person pointed to the chopper just as the door opened and a beautiful lady-bird pilot popped out. "Come on aboard, handsome," she said. "You're gonna fly higher than anybody in this forest—and in your own plane!"

"Don't worry about flying," the Tall Person chimed in. "Sing, record, and if it sells, those residuals will see that you fly."

STUNG

Tom "Flaps" Kelly loved to fly anything and everything. As a kid, he made airplanes out of balsa wood; then he turned to the model kits, which had pieces you put together to make planes that could fly. He started with the rubber-band types, and then tried the ones with a tiny engine. When he was fifteen years old, Flaps flew his first biplane, a two-seater, the kind that's scarce today and are usually used to spray insecticides. By the time World War II raged, Flaps had become a fighter pilot; he downed eight Messerschmitts over France. When he came home and settled in northern California, Flaps, not surprisingly, decided to become a pilot for a big company. (Well, actually, it was a little company that the big company was going to buy.)

Tom and his wife came to live on a small ranch, about fifty acres, in the Santa Ynez Valley. One warm, sunny day Flaps got a call to come over to the airfield to see some new plane. As he was pulling his old 1955 convertible Buick out of the barn a bumblebee stung him right in the ear. Poor Flaps let out a yell that spun the weather vane around on top of the barn. When he glanced in the car's mirror, he saw his face was puffed like a wrestler's. But a job was a job, so he drove on anyway.

Just as he was about to pull into the airfield, it happened again: a swarm of honeybees flew right into his face. Flaps swerved to the right, almost totaling the car, and went off into a Cyclone fence. The bees stung him on the chest so much it looked as if he had either a small pillow under his shirt or the beginning of a huge goiter.

Somehow, Lord knows how, he pulled himself together and strolled into the hangar. The president of the company greeted him. "Flaps, you old bastard. Remember me, Colonel Ballsteder? I was your squadron commander in England."

"Course I do," Flaps replied as they shook hands.

They went into the hangar and popped a couple of beers. Then came the briefing; Ballsteder filled Flaps in on the experimental plane he wanted him to fly. "I know you're not checked out in jets like this, but it'll all come back to you."

Flaps changed into his old flight suit, helmet, goggles and boots. He even pinned his old wings on. A lot of years had gone by, but even with gray hair Flaps had maintained the same trim weight he'd had in the Air Corps during the war. And with the mustache he had added, Flaps actually looked more like a wing commander in the RAF than an American flyboy.

Just before he went out to the plane, Flaps hesitantly approached Ballsteder. If it wasn't too much trouble, he asked, he could use an advance on his salary; his little ranch wasn't producing because of water problems and he could really use the cash.

His old colonel laughed and jammed a check into Flaps's leather glove. "You clown, here's the whole damn check, fifteen thousand dollars," he said. "Now, go out and fly that son of a bitch!"

Flaps sauntered out to the shiny new aircraft and climbed in, and when the ground crew pulled away the chocks, he kicked over the engine. He whipped her around, taxied, got his signal from the tower and took off. As he swiftly climbed to his altitude, Ballsteder's check fell from his pocket; as he picked it up Flaps saw that it had "void" written on its back. Once again, on the same day, he'd been stung.

To hell with it, Flaps cursed; he was a pro, he'd fulfill his end of the bargain. He turned his aluminum bastard everywhere but loose. He went through all kinds of rolls, loops, dives, turns, stall-outs, you name it. Just before landing, he decided to try some low-altitude cruising; he was only fifty feet above ground when he got a glimpse, a blur, of a great-looking blonde coming out of a joint called—you're not going to believe this—the Bumblebee Bar. Flaps shot straight up and was coming back for another pass at this incredible creature when all of a sudden his engine flamed out; the jet screamed straight into Bumblebee Mountain.

The blonde raced across an open field when she saw Flaps crash; there she stood, numbed by what she saw, still carrying her drink from the bar, a stinger.

Miraculously, Flaps, near death, was thrown almost a hundred yards from the wreckage; he landed right in the center of a group of abandoned beehives. Flaps opened his eyes one last time, perhaps it was a reflex, and saw in the sky above him a plane, a skywriter, spelling out B-U-Z-Z-Z-Z.

MY LAST
FLIGHT SOUTH

I understand a lot of people enjoy escaping from the icy winds and heavy snows of the north. Well, we ducks also look forward to flying south for the winter.

Like our friends the great Canadian geese, we fly in a V shape; how high is anybody's guess. But rest assured, we always try to fly out of range of those hunters who bang away at us from their blinds.

It was last fall, a little later than usual, that about a hundred of us took off from some lakes in northern Michigan and headed south. Although the sky was crystal clear, it was definitely cold. We were glad to be leaving the pond and what was left of some rushes.

Food was really getting scarce. We took off shortly before dawn. It seemed to me there was an unnecessary amount of quacking. Being the leader, I told everybody to hold it down; we could all celebrate when we finally got to Mexico, or, better yet, Central America.

The earth looked cold and just as bare as it did the year before. There were only vestiges of cornstalks, stubble or alfalfa and the trees were bare. A very heavy frost covered the ground, making it look as if there was almost an inch of snow on the ground.

We crossed over a wide and very long river, probably the Ohio. When we had been flying at least three hours, I spotted a fair-sized pond in what I had to believe was northern Kentucky. I headed in first, as I was the leader. I was about fifty feet off the water when I heard a loud bang. That's all, but it was over just like that. I fell like a rock into the icy waters below. If there were other shots, I didn't hear them.

The next thing I knew, I was staring into the eyes of a black Labrador retriever. He was coming to pick me up. Ever been in a dog's mouth? Interestingly enough, they're rather gentle. They know you're dead, so they don't hurt you. I was still barely alive when this big black head moved toward me with a wide-open mouth.

Just before he clamped down on me, I told him I was not just an ordinary duck. I was a redheaded canvasback, all right, but I was a "fish eater." He stopped dead in his tracks, slammed on the brakes (hard to do in deep water), gave me a wink, and circled back to the duck blind. He saved himself some extra paddling, but missed out on a big pat on the head.

Me, I died, all right, but with dignity. Sure, I got shot down. I don't care what anybody says, in the long run it still pays to eat fish.

FACES

A long, long time ago, when I was quite small, I saw a number of faces—mostly of fellow animals, and some birds. I don't remember many people's faces, perhaps because we lived so very far back in the bush.

If anyone was guilty of staring, it would be me— many a day I would just stretch out and look as far as I could look. I watched all kinds of faces, and they, in turn, would stare at me.

When I went off with my family we would scour miles and miles of terrain in search of food. I was in on a number of kills but rarely did I look at their faces.

Now that I'm in America, all day long, from 10 A.M. until 5 P.M., I see nothing but people's faces—children and their parents, aunts, uncles, who all seem to be carrying small black things that a light flashes on from. I can't make out what they're saying, but I certainly understand their expressions, their eyes, their faces. The expression on my face is always the same; on occasion I show my teeth and growl. With all these people visiting the zoo I never really can remember a face for very long. What *is* strange is that I've never seen any of the other animals or the birds in the zoo. I probably never will. We're all kept separate for some reason. Strange. We managed to get along so well—for the most part—in the jungle.

How strange it is that I've never seen *my* face. I have seen it, of course, when I drink a little water. I just have really never seen my face the way I'd like to see it, the way those who stare at me see it. Funny, we tigers have an old saying about ourselves, "Don't we all look alike!" Those kids and adults, they certainly look different, all different colors, shapes, sizes, some tall and some short. They never seem to look at each other's faces. Maybe when they feed they look at each other's faces. I'm glad we all look alike, we don't have to stare at each other's face. We know what we look like.

If you ask me, the best time to stare is when you're thinking about mating. That's how I ended up in this zoo—it was the mating season, and I was staring at her and she was staring at me. I might add that since we've been in the zoo we've never mated again.

CHILDREN'S
VOICES

A BLINDING
SNOWSTORM

According to Granddad, it's really snowing outside—he said it was a "blinding snowstorm." How will Dad ever get home? I'll bet those old windshield wipers of his can't make it through this stuff.

Well, they got the tree up, an eight-footer, right, Mom? How you doin' with the decorations? Can I help you with the lights? Grandma's out in the kitchen —I can smell that cookin' in here, cookies, biscuits, bread, stuffing, pies. Gosh! I love Christmas!

Somebody, turn the TV on. I'll bet you anything *A Christmas Carol* is on; surely it's on *one* of the stations.

I like Christmas Eve the best of all. Sis is still upstairs wrapping presents, and knowing her, she'll be up all night. (Wish I could wrap presents like Mom does. She does the best. It always seems a shame to tear all that paper up, it's so pretty.)

And Big Puss over there by the fire, that fat old cat, I can't remember his ever being outside any time of the year. Matter of fact, I've never seen him go after a mouse. But don't he look pretty with that big red bow around his neck? And Bozo—he's going on seventeen this spring—why don't they let him in? If anybody would take it bad during a blinding snowstorm, it would be Bozo.

Everything looks so beautiful—the tree, the stockings hung by the chimney, Grandma's new hooked rug. I suppose it's stupid to worry about all the birds and animals and folks who are out there in that blinding snowstorm. How can they see to even get across the street?

Wait, here's my old teddy bear, Pooh. Come to think of it, I've had him since I was four, and now I'm almost seventeen. For seventeen Christmases, I've been looking at all these beautiful things in this big, beautiful living room, in this old house. Doc Turner said this would probably be the last Christmas that I would see. The four operations didn't work. It's terrible to be blind, but at Christmas it's really rough. Thank God I'll be able to hear the carols, smell the crackling fire, listen to Granddad snore, smell Grandma's cooking, and know when Mom and Dad are laughing and swinging each other about.

What's that, Granddad? Oh, I'm just going outside for a couple of minutes; thought I'd start to get used to a blinding snowstorm.

WHAT DO YOU WANT TO BE
WHEN YOU GROW UP?

What do you want to be when you grow up, Johnny?

I want to be a pilot, a fighter pilot, and I want to be the leader of my squadron. The enemy will hide behind the clouds when they see me!

I want to be a doctor and help kids get well, old people walk, deliver babies and make a young husband and wife smile.

I want to grow up to be a daddy, play with my children, be there to tuck them in at night and tell them a story.

I want to be a great artist when I grow up, so the

president of the United States will commission me to paint him, with all the important people coming to the unveiling.

I want to receive the Medal of Honor for bravery. For leading a charge, for saving my men, for keeping our flag waving above us and for turning back thousands of the enemy against incredible odds.

I want to grow up to be a movie star, with women of all ages throwing themselves at my feet. Everywhere I go, girls will scream and yell. I'll only have to do two big pictures a year and be paid so much money that the rest of the year I can play; I'll have a classy sports car and a huge home.

I want to be president of the United States. I will be all things to all people. I won't lie and I'll be honest with everybody.

I want to be a great comedian and make people laugh. It feels so good to laugh. How many people say, "You know, I don't know when I laughed as much as I did last night." I want to be funny, really funny.

Here I am, an old man. You know something? All the things I mentioned—I'm still unsure about the answers to the question. You know why? It's simple: I forgot to grow up!

Why did I forget to grow up?

THE MIRAGE

The old house was big and old, but, oh, so warm inside. Almost every room was filled with laugher. Mom and Dad were always there—at least it seemed that way. If any of us had any kind of problems or we came down with some kind of illness—they were there. Sometimes we would have problems with our studies, and if Dad couldn't help us, Mom did. Oh the *love* that was in that big old house!

We were never lonely—we all loved one another and there were a lot of us. And each of us had a dog or a kitty to play with. And oh so many, many toys!

We had a number of chores to take care of, but we all pitched in and it made things easy.

If I could think of a flaw, it would be that all of us had so much to do in that old house that none of us ever really wanted to go out into the outside world.

Oh heck! Who am I kidding? It's all a mirage. There's no mom and dad here at St. Gustav's Orphanage.

I WAS BEHIND THE COUCH
ALL THE TIME

I've long had the impression that you get educated in school. Grade school, especially, but kindergarten first, then high school and later, hopefully, in college. Learning to read and write is essential, but the best courses are always found outside school. Outside is where you really learn—in a factory, cutting trees for lumber, picking fruit, working in the wheat fields, shucking corn, pumping gas, selling ties, being an inspector in a Coca-Cola bottling plant, laying pipe, packing hay in a barn, putting in posts on a farm, stacking iron stoves for Buckeye Incubator Co., washing trucks, even playing Santa Claus at Christmastime.

The whole world is a magnificent classroom, I often say; the problem is that too many people are out for recess. For me, aside from American history and art contests and going abroad, I got the bulk of my education about people, voices, history, sex, gossip and family from behind the couch.

Being an only child does automatically make you a loner, a survivor, one hell of a listener, a person who is sensitive, somewhat paranoid, full of curiosity, and able to entertain himself or herself for long periods of time. Don't misunderstand: friends are always essential, but don't ever give me the line about counting them on one hand; how about one finger?

For the first seventeen years of my life I spent a lot of time behind the couch. And I did listen! What an eye-opener one can get just from two men and two women sitting on an old Victorian couch with a few faded throw pillows on it. But to list all the things I listened to would fill a book, and much of it might be terribly boring. The fun for me came years later. I waited like a great cat, well into my twenties, to spring from behind the couch on all of those people who had counted me out. I acted out their lives, their decisions, right in front of them. I was holding up this huge mirror, this golden frame, that I placed around this frightening family portrait.

I'm not one to preach, but, you know, it wouldn't hurt to hide behind that couch of yours. You'll get the opportunity to study and listen to those who sit on it. Even though I'm almost sixty, I find myself still hiding, but as I look back (and I do now more than ever), I'm glad I was behind the couch all the time.

One last thing: as for *lying on* a couch, take it from me that whatever you do, the only time you want to be there is to read or sleep. If there's a man sitting in a chair with a writing tablet and a pencil in his hands, forget it—tell him you do *your* interviews sitting up.

DR. JOHN WOOKEY
TO SURGERY

Eight operations in one day is a lot of operations—
at least, I think so. I'd just come out of my last one, a
two-hour job, not terribly complex, but mean, difficult
to get to. What's more, wouldn't you know it, my
anesthesiologist was off on vacation. And my two
nurses? They were always primping, combing their
hair and talking about boys and how their parents
were so stupid about so many things, and did they
really want to be nurses after all?

When I looked around my operating room, I realized I just couldn't go on operating this way. Certainly if I was going to continue to save lives I needed

much better facilities and more up-to-date equipment. I needed the right instruments—can you imagine operating with a Swiss Army knife? Illumination? All I had above the operating table was three huge flashlights tied together with a string. I needed sponges too, and you wouldn't believe how hard they are to find. My recovery room? It was a joke: just a couple of orange crates pushed together with an old ironing board that belonged to my grandmother. And having to scrub up in the garage—the pits.

All this was on my mind as I was finally removing my surgeon's cap and apron, and slipping out of my faded aqua gown. I suddenly realized that Billy, my next-door neighbor, was standing in back of me and crying. I noticed he was holding a small pasted cardboard box with several holes in the top. Slowly he opened the lid, and there inside was a large toad.

"What's the problem, Billy?" I asked. "What can I do for you? Better yet, what can I do for your toad?"

"Ya gotta take his warts off, Doc," he cried. "I think they're really hurtin' him!"

I was going to take the toad's temperature, but I remembered I was missing a thermometer. I figured I might as well stall by taking a history. "What's the toad's name, Billy?"

"Mr. Puff," he replied, " 'Cause he's always puffed up."

I thought for a moment. "I can give you a quick diagnosis, Billy. Mr. Puff is a North American toad, so his warts are natural, and they are there for a reason—they camouflage him. Okay, Billy?"

He seemed relieved and almost started to smile. "I'd just take him out of that box and let him get some fresh air," I continued, "and by the way, my fee is twenty-five cents."

HOW MUCH MONEY
DID YOU MAKE TODAY,
LITTLE MAN?

How much money did you make today, little man? Only fifteen cents. I sold an old green bottle I found buried out back of the barn.

How much money did you make today, little man? Carried some groceries, four big bags of them, for an old woman to her car. She gave me a whole quarter.

How much money did you make today, little man? I raked leaves all day long for Mr. Rodgers, took them in an old dirty sheet down to Buck Creek and burned them. Both my hands are sore and full of blisters. Mr. Rodgers gave me a dollar, a silver dollar, said he'd had it for a long time.

How much money did you make today, little man? I washed Grandpa's pickup and then waxed it, made it look almost new. Grandpa gave me seventy-five cents and a picture of him in uniform when he was in World War I.

How much money did you make today, little man? I shoveled snow all day Saturday and most of Sunday. Would have made a bunch of money but the handle broke. As it was, I almost made two bucks.

How much money did you make today, little man? I didn't make a cent today—hard to believe, ain't it? I've been hustling ever since I was born. But today I found something better than money. Something I've been looking for a long, long time, ever since my dad died. No, it ain't money. I found a friend, a real friend, somebody that don't care whether I got money or not. Last thing she said to me today was, "I don't care how much you made today, little man. I love you and just want to be your wife!" It's not to say she doesn't love me; I'm sure she does and I love her, but we're only kids and I'll bet you anything when I grow up and do marry her, first thing she's going to say is, "How much money did you make today, little man?"

A LITTLE BOY'S
CHRISTMAS LIST

I sure hope we have another big Christmas tree with all the lights and stuff on it. And my stocking—I hope it has a little more in it, last year it was only half full. Every year I ask Santa for a train, but I never get one; that book on trains Uncle Ray gave me isn't the same.

I hope Aunt Lou doesn't give me another scarf. The guys always say it looks like a girl's. I'd sure like a *Star Wars* costume but Wally, the kid up the block, said they were all bought up before Thanksgiving.

I asked Santa in my letter if he'd make Grandpa well enough to come downstairs for Christmas Eve. I wonder sometimes the way the mails are if my letter really gets to the North Pole. I seem to be the only one in the house that writes to Santa. Santa, if you hear me, could you find it in your heart to give me a real good set of ear plugs. I just can't stand to hear Sis's rock albums any longer.

Oh, by the way, Santa, would you send me Mr. Robert's book, *Math Can Be Fun*? I really don't want it (I hate math), but now that I'm in the third grade I'm desperate.

I also need a new fishing reel, Santa. The old one's okay, understand, but Dad says next spring if everything goes okay, just him and me are going way up to Canada, where the big ones are, so I don't want to take a chance of losin' that big one.

Santa, do you ever give those big silver dollars Grandpa used to get? If it's worn, I don't care. I know Dad carries one for good luck. I'd put mine in a secret hiding place.

You know something also I'd like, Santa? It isn't necessary, but I could do with a new pair of mittens, sheepskin-lined. My wool ones are shot. They don't have to be expensive, just real warm!

Santa, I know I'm not allowed to come downstairs on Christmas Eve when you fill the stockings, but would you do me one small favor and let me hear your sleigh bells when you take off from the roof?

My room is way at the other end of the house, so you gotta ring 'em real loud!

Santa, I realize you've got so many things to think about, and so much to deliver to kids all over the world, but you know the two things I would settle for more than anything? That every poor kid gets a wonderful toy—one that no one else has—and a wonderful Christmas dinner. And I know you'll laugh at this, but you know what I really want from Dad? I want for him to pick me up, kiss me and tell me he loves me. (Mom does it, but I guess Dad forgets!)

Santa, before I forget it, I'm gonna make you a promise, one that goes for you, too, Mrs. Santa Claus, and all the elves: I'll cut my list down to just five things. Oh, and by the way, if you should give me that fishing reel, I'm sure Dad would let you go along with us to Canada to go fishing. Besides, I'd really like to get to know you, when you're not working. You know kids all over the world love you. By the way, how do you go around the world in one night?

A BABY-SITTER
AND WHY THEY'RE WEIRD
OR TURN WEIRD

Ever watch a little boy or a little girl (or both) for eight hours or more? Well, this is one of the reasons I drank. Don't misunderstand. I loved my son and daughter when they were little and I love them even more now. But how well I remember saying: "Don't touch that figurine, it'll break. Don't pull the dog's tail; don't wind the big clock on the wall backwards. Why? Because it's not supposed to be wound backwards, only forwards. Besides, *I* just wound it. Don't put kitty's head in the hot bowl of soup. Why? Because cats don't eat soup. Don't paint Grandfather's picture green. Why? Because it won't come off and,

besides, *he's* not green. Why are you standing on top
of the house? Please come down right now, okay?
You won't come down until I buy you a new Frisbee?
Well, I won't buy you one, and if you don't come
down right away I'll hire a child hit man to shoot you
down! Don't swing on the living room drapes! Why?
Because you're too heavy—as a matter of fact, you're
fat and you'll not only pull the drapes down, but
probably a good portion of the ceiling. Don't strangle
your sister! Why? It seems to me, and it should to
you, that you'll kill her! You say she doesn't love you?
Well, release her—release your grip and I'm sure she'll
tell you she does. Why are you banging that hammer
on the refrigerator door? You saw a man do this in a
commercial on TV? Well, the model we have is obviously not the same as the one you saw in the commercial because it's ruined. Why *did* you do it? Why?
Because you didn't like your paintings or crayon
drawings we put up? Why did you drink all the
liquor in Daddy's liquor cabinet? That's very dangerous and it could kill you. Why do I drink it? Because
of medicinal reasons—that and it's none of your damn
business. Why have you painted those weird pictures
in your room? I know it's *your* room, but we—your
mother and I just wallpapered it a month ago; now it
will take you the rest of your life to pay to have it

done over. Why did you leave the faucet running in your bathroom? Because it sounds like the falls you saw last summer? Why did you use the telephone all day and almost all night Saturday? What was that? You say you wanted Tommy to help you with the instructions for the model airplane? Why couldn't he come over here? He's five doors away from us. You know between you and your sisters using the one telephone in the house our telephone bill is over three hundred dollars a month? Why did you take the spikes out of my golf shoes? Because you wanted them to look like the rest of my shoes! Why did you let the parakeets out of the cage? You read where they come back at night? Well, they don't—believe me, they don't *ever* come back. Why did you take the four goldfish out of their bowl, wrap them in Kleenex and put them in your bed? What? You say they were still swimming around and it was 10 P.M. and so you made them go to bed? Why did you take my gold pen and pencil and put them in a skillet and melt them down? You wanted to make a gold coin—is that it? Why did you paint our telephone red? Because the president's is and it's the hot line, and you thought it would make *you* feel important?"

The baby-sitter's job is a tough job—one should really put cotton in one's ears. Heavy sedation helps.

A baby-sitter should hide in a room in the house and stay there until the parents come home. Hide-and-seek is always a fun game and keeps the children occupied—only you make sure you have *all* the keys to all the doors.

Booze is used by a number of baby-sitters, but it's dangerous because often the baby-sitter will go to sleep, burn up the house or let the children run out into the night. A truly great baby-sitter is a great hypnotist, who, if her or she is any good at all, can put the children in a deep trance and lay them out on the couch or balance them on an ironing board.

THE
COSTUME

It was a very cold day as I looked through the frosted windows in my room. Outside, there was snow as far as you could see. A few trees stood out, as did some bushes. I always stayed inside on days like this and Mom always brought me my meals. She was one hell of a cook and, it goes without saying, one of the dearest people I ever knew.

I'd been sick most of my life and now my condition was worsening. Over the past year, my temper was giving me a lot of problems. I was throwing things, banging my head against the walls in my room, and tore up some pretty thick books I'd had. The medicine

Doc Fuller was giving me wasn't working anymore. He knew it and so did I. I remember my dad saying: "The boy isn't right—he never has been and he never will be."

One of the things I liked to do was dress up and pretend I was different people. I had a fair-sized closet full of costumes. Today being so cold outside, I decided I'd dress up again.

I was sitting on the edge of my bed eating a bologna sandwich and drinking a glass of milk. Mom was sitting alongside my bed in a beat-up old wing chair my grandfather used to sit in. I was watching a war movie on television—it was a picture about Vietnam. And when I quietly finished my sandwich and my milk, I went over to my closet. In a couple of minutes, I was completely dressed as a combat veteran, camouflaged from head to toe. I went into my bathroom, opened my medicine chest and went through my makeup tubes.

When I came out, Mom had gone. I began to feel funny—my mind was playing games with me again. I broke a window and stuck an old broom handle through it, and pretended I was firing on the enemy. Then I sat down to cry. I don't know why. I just sat down and cried.

Mom and two men came into the room. The men were both in white and for a minute I thought they were covered with snow.

Mom sat down on the edge of the bed. She'd brought up a big plate of cookies and offered them to the men and then to me. One of the men asked to see my collection of costumes. I looked over at Mom, a kind of seeking-approval look, and she nodded. The man took his time going through them, then slowly turned and said, "You got some kind of costumes here, my friend. You must've been collecting for a long, long time."

Then the other man, a big, big black man, said, "We gotta costume for you, bet ya don't have it." It wasn't like any of my costumes; it was all open from the back and had lots of straps. The two men helped me slip it on, and then I sat down in Grandfather's chair. Mom whispered a lot of things in my ear and kissed me a couple of times on the cheek. Then I left with the two men, one of whom had a whole bunch of my costumes draped over his arm. He told me that if I got well, I could wear my old costumes, but for now my new costume would have to do.

Mom wrote me later that on the day I left with those men, she couldn't tell us apart because we were all wearing white. I still don't like wintertime. I miss Mom's sandwiches and those cold glasses of milk, but at least it's warm where I'm at and they let me keep my costumes.

WHAT ARE YOU
FRIGHTENED OF, JOHNNY?

"What are you frightened of, Johnny?"
I'm frightened of that cloud that's over Russia.
I'm scared of war between Libya and us.
I'm really scared of Chubby Davis—that bully that beats up on me and lives two doors away from us.
I'm afraid I'm not gonna pass into the next grade come June.
I'm frightened of lightning—last summer lightning struck the big pine tree in our front yard. Grandpa said it was more than two hundred years old.
I'm afraid of Mrs. Pavick's pit bull—he bit my

hand when I reached through the fence to get my baseball.

I'm afraid we'll never have peace—we might maybe for a while but not for very long.

I'm frightened and scared that Mom and Dad will die someday and I'll be all alone.

I'm scared to put my newspaper money in the bank 'cause it was held up a couple of weeks ago.

You know what really frightened me the most? Mom and Dad—'cause they drink every night, and though they never beat me they're always saying they never shoulda had me.

Everybody I know is scared of God. I ain't, I figure he's the one person might be scared himself—well, now and then. After all, he's only human.

OF MEN AND WAR

THE BLUE HILL
MASSACRE

Anytime you have to fight in a war, it's bad, very bad. And to have to fight in the wintertime is probably the worst.

The temperatures that day on Blue Hill had dropped to twenty below. I swear, the only things warm were the cannons, the rifles and one huge fire.

I don't know how many other skirmishes I had fought against General von Hauser. He was a crafty old fox; I called him the Weasel. He would strike, advance a few thousand yards and then disappear into thin air. This particular winter day, though, I had the old Weasel finally pinned down with his back against the wall.

My artillery had really done a job on von Hauser. With the exception of about a dozen companies, his men had all fallen. In the past he was always able to count on supplies coming to his aid, but not in today's cold—nothing could get through. I looked at the old general through my field glasses, or what was left of them; one of the lenses must have fallen out sometime during the battle. But it didn't matter; I could still make him out—a tall man, six feet four, who wore a monocle in his right eye. Suddenly, he fell to his knees. With his right hand, he pulled a white scarf from around his neck and began to wave it, first to the left, and then to the right. Had the old Weasel really given up? Or was he pulling one last trick? Of all the battles I'd been in with the general, I could never recall his waving the white flag.

But now, incredibly, he meant it.

So the Blue Hill Massacre had come to an end, and I, General Fillmore Harrison, United States 2nd Artillery, Rainbow Division, had all but leveled General Ernst von Hauser and the German Army's 1st Artillery. Another war had ended. As we got to our feet— one old retired American general and one old retired German general—we made our way over to the huge fireplace in our old family home in Blue Hill, Connecticut. We raised our drinks, toasted to peace, took a long look out through the huge bay window at the softly falling snow and then gazed down at our armies all scattered about on the Persian rug. The soldiers were strewn everywhere. The general's white scarf was draped over a large leather chair. Slowly, we both bent down and began to put our troops back in their respective boxes.

THE
REBELS

It wasn't that we had known one another all our lives, because we hadn't. It just seemed that way because we did have one thing in common: we had been in a war and we were all badly wounded. Although we were from different parts of the country and in different outfits—Army, Navy, Marines—we were all discharged from the same VA hospital. We had labeled ourselves the Rebels. I was Hawk, an airborne. Sergeant had lost both hands trying to detonate a land mine; "Gunner" was blinded by an explosion on a patrol boat in the Mekong Delta, Vietnam; and last, but not least, Bronco, a marine first sergeant, had been deafened in both ears by heavy bombardments on his bunker on the DMZ in Vietnam. Why were we rebels? Not just because we'd been hit badly, it was *how* we handled our disabilities. For instance, Hawk, who had nothing left below his wrists, spent six days a week going to a local beauty parlor getting his fingernails done on his plastic hands. As for Gunner, blind, he would go from one optometrist to another, places where they fitted you for glasses and go through all kinds of different tests. Bronco, the deaf marine, wore two hearing aids and was always going into places like record shops or the Radio Shack and making the salesmen turn everything up "so he could hear it."

We four men now shared an apartment. We were often asked by our parents, friends, sweethearts, "What are you going to do with your lives?" And our answer was, "We gave half of our lives to our country, the rest belongs to us. We want to be rebels. We don't want to conform anymore."

I WANT TO BE
A SOLDIER

I want to be a soldier and wear a handsome uniform.

I'll be brave, and if I'm wounded I'll still fight and fight until I die.

If I'm an officer, my men will follow me and respect me because I will have come up through the ranks—I'll be one of them.

I will give orders and I will take orders. I'll question things from time to time, but in the end I will carry out the orders that have been given to me.

I will kill the enemy every chance I get—I will show no mercy, for I know he will never show me any. There will be no prisoners, no exchanges, no interrogations.

For it is a war we are in; blast the treaties! To hell with white flags! We will win, we will win, victory will be ours!

When we write home we will write only of victories.

If by chance we are defeated, let us all be smiling at the enemy—singing—holding our swords and rifles high above our heads. Remember, we are not dying for our country, our families at home. For God? Maybe!

Oh, no, my comrades, we in our lovely uniforms are not dying for some "cause." Certainly age has nothing to do with it. Here I am, a captain, all of thirty-one. It certainly has nothing to do with my ten years of training. Are we all that dedicated? Hell, no! let us take a good long look at ourselves, lads, this is all we *can* do—*kill*! Ah, but look at the bright side— should we win (and we *will* win, you know), think of that great parade we'll be in when we come home. Everybody at home loves a good parade.

Lads, I've just received word we're out of ammunition. Let us all form one long line, give one hell of a scream and dash toward the enemy. Of course, we'll die—the parade, I'm afraid, is off. But those bastards that will be mowing us down will never forget us and how brave we were. Of course, we'll be considered fools at home. But then, lads, war *is* only for fools. The enemy will win *this* time, but, mark my word, a taste of victory many times can make you an even bigger fool. 'Nough said! Bugler! "Charge, you crazy bastards, *charge!*"

THE IVY-COVERED
CASTLE

Once upon a time, somewhere in the English countryside, probably in the west, was a beautiful ivy-covered castle called, appropriately enough, Ivy Castle. Centuries later the ivy died and the place became known as Grey Castle. The knight who owned and lived in the castle was known as Allan the Badger of Willowwood, Sovereignshire of Moofley. Allan wanted more than anything to be a king, king of all England and, if not England, at least a desolate part of northern Scotland.

So to win over the people and hopefully topple King Henry, he galloped through all the surrounding villages, giving each poor person a goose and a gold crown. He told them they were welcome to live in his castle but they would have to keep it clean, scrub the turrets, shine the chains on the drawbridge and always be merry. They would also have to feed the people of the castle by growing and selling the huge mass of watercress that surrounded the moat.

All the villagers, once they entered the castle, were immediately given costumes of friars and nuns. The reason was simple. You see, at this time in England, it was an unwritten law that the enemy could never, never kill friars or nuns.

But one terrible winter night a huge army of soldiers, along with merchants and fierce animals, stormed the castle. The soldiers were from Persia and, of course, they had no idea what nuns and friars were, so they slaughtered them all. After all heads were counted and placed on farm tools, the infidels turned the castle into a great hotel with exotic foods, unusual soft drinks, fake tobacco and lots of belly dancers. As for Allan the Badger, he was spared but was made a prisoner and forced to live in the castle's dungeon. His only therapy was to construct pillows out of straw. He kept his humor and sanity by constantly talking to himself and speaking in tongues; being an Anglican, he could speak in eighteen of them.

At the ripe old age of eighty-seven, Allan was finally released by the Persians. He had little money, so he set out on foot for Lisbon. Here he came upon a male witch who taught him how to cook exotic Arabian and Persian dishes, plus some unusual Congolese desserts with just a hint of poison. He soon returned to his castle and successfully applied for the job of head chef and cooked for his conquerors. Within a period of ninety days they all died of, of all things, a poison gas that developed in day-old cabbages.

Today, this very castle, once more called Grey Castle, is again a hotel, an inn and discotheque often frequented by Arab terrorists.

I STAND ALONE

Most of my life I was alone—as a child and all through school.

I must admit I truly enjoyed being by myself.

But not today—today I dread being alone.

I've been in two wars and half a dozen campaigns.

I'd never had a brother or a sister. It was only at the front and in the trenches that I met my brothers.

First I fought alongside them, bled with them, sang and drank and cried with them.

Yes, I even led them and finally died with them.

During those wars and campaigns I was never alone except once.

I was cut off from my outfit for three days behind enemy lines.

I wasn't afraid of the enemy, the thought of being captured or even being killed.

It was being *alone*—away from my men, my brothers that really frightened me most of all.

I spent some time in a field hospital and while I was there the nurses—thank God for them—with their quiet voices, their cheery hellos, an occasional kiss on the cheek, that soft hand on my forehead—these angels in white became my sisters.

My rest, convalescence, was all too short.

My wounds were slight and so it was back to the front.

I was a general now—the most decorated man in the cavalry, perhaps any cavalry in the world.

It wasn't the decorations or the fact that I was a general—a hero.

I was back with my men—my brothers.

I was mounted on a beautiful white charger, the rain was coming down in torrents.

But the men, my men, were singing all around me. Those on horseback and even the foot soldiers. They were singing for many reasons—chiefly because we were all together and this was our last campaign—

and then home. The whole regiment going home together!

Suddenly shell fire, rifle shots, cannon, screaming, horses rearing up, everywhere men scattering, looking for cover. And then I felt a sharp pain in my chest and I slumped from my horse onto the muddy, rain-soaked road. We were all being massacred, wiped out —ambushed!

A corporal dragged me to a smoldering stump. He put his canteen up to my lips, the cold water sloshed about in my hot mouth momentarily and then trickled out the corners.

Then a captain knelt by my side, then two privates, then another and another. The whole regiment seemed to be around me. Even my horse made his way over and the reins fell across the palm of my hand.

We were all going home together, after all. My brothers—the only ones I'd ever known—we were going home for good this time.

I shall always remember the singing, and as muddy as the roads had been and as cold and drenched as we were, we suddenly—all of us—looked very clean. For a moment—I would've sworn that the sun had come out. Then it became very dark—black.

Today I stand alone—no horse, no men, no singing, nothing!

Except it's raining again and I'm in a little town. A ghost town whose inhabitants have all been evacuated. It's another war—another time.

And I'm just a statue—the only statue in this little town.

OBSERVATIONS

WE'RE GOING OUT FOR
TWO WHOLE DAYS

Do you know what it's like to be inside for five long years? Or even a year?

Even if it's sunny outside, when you do see the sun, I swear it looks gray. The whole damn place is gray. All of us are gray.

But we're going out into the countryside for two whole days. Think of it. Sure, we'll be watched, many of us are considered dangerous. Still . . . just to see wildflowers, to feel a tree, maybe even climb it; they say there's a creek where we'll be allowed to swim, *maybe*. (Everything is maybe. *Maybe* you'll be going home next spring. *Maybe* you can make one call home.

Maybe you'll be leaving here *forever* someday . . . *maybe!*)

I hope today we really, not maybe, are going out into the country. Oh God, suppose it rains? But it doesn't. And now a dozen of us are going—six men, six women—and four of them to watch us. Even the bus ride out is a treat because of all the things you've seen so many times before but which suddenly become so important. Gas stations, bus stops, grocery stores, people, children, cars, streets, freeways, buildings, housing projects, trees, flowers and a dog chasing a cat.

One of the women starts to cry. She tells me she was born on a farm and talks about her mom and dad, milking cows, gathering eggs, and feeding the chickens. She cries and cries. And when we make it out into the country, she stays on the bus.

The first thing we do is spread out some blankets in this big open field so they can feed us our picnic— some hard-boiled eggs and bologna and cheese sandwiches on white. When one guy asks for rare roast beef on rye, one of "them" lets out a roar of laughter. The guy finds a fresh "meadow muffin" (some hot cow dung), and lets him have it right in the face. Two of "them" grab the guy, put something in his mouth, a tablet, maybe two, and tie him to one of the seats on the bus. I look over at the bus, the big gray bus. And I look at the guy. He's twistin' and turnin' somethin' fierce. I'm sure he's just kidding, trying to be funny, but who knows.

Somebody says, "Let's play softball," so we start playing. I played ball in high school and in the service. I'd show these gray freaks that I can drive that ball over the red barn, I want to show those sickos I can do it. As I hold the bat, I notice all of "them" looking uneasy. To *me*, I'm just holding a beat-up old Louisville slugger. Well, I don't even get on base. I strike out, as a matter of fact. I'm depressed.

I ask one of "them" if I can go swimming. He nods, so I slip out of my gray pants and jump in the creek. It must be spring water, since I almost freeze my balls off. I'm in the creek for about an hour when one of the women comes over. She bends down and I put a crawdad in her hair. She goes bananas. They take her to the bus and chain her to a seat too.

Two of "them" come over to me and say, "Get your butt outa the creek." Then they work me over pretty good. I go over to a dead tree and sit down against it. Suddenly, I hear giggling from inside the dead tree. I look around and a man and woman are making out.

The day goes by quickly.

It's the most fun I've had in all the time I've been in the place, but we're told by "them" that we didn't live up to *their* standards of behavior. There will be no more picnics.

Somebody, not any of us, took a picture of us all. (A bunch of "nuts" out in the country for two whole days!) One of "them" says that *maybe* we'd all get a copy of it. Maybe.

Well, we just got the picture, and wouldn't you know it? It's not even in color; they'd never spend that kind of bread. But the picture is out of focus, anyway, just a shade out and . . . gray.

WHAT IT MUST'VE BEEN LIKE

What the creek must've been like when it was clear and you could see the crawdads movin' slowly on the sandy bottom!

What it must've been like swingin' on that old used tire across the creek. That old tire, as worn as it was, held us all, fat or skinny. So did that rope and that old limb.

What it must've been like to see that field of wheat swayin' back and forth on that hot July day with just enough of a breeze to make it move.

What it must've been like to walk down that narrow gravel road from the main house to the mailbox.

What it must've been like to look up in that blue sky and see a biplane fly over. There was no jet trail then, just a cough every once and a while and a sputter.

What it must've been like to see the pilot wave back at you with his goggles—you in a pair of faded overalls and bare feet.

I wonder what it must've been like to have all the fireworks you wanted on the Fourth of July?

I wonder what it must've been like to go with the whole family in Grandfather's old Packard on Sunday. (The Packard with the "wooden spokes.")

I wonder what it must've been like to pick a big beefsteak tomato out in the garden and wash it off in the creek.

I wonder what it was like to talk with my black friend Booker T, with no one giving it a second thought.

I wonder what it was like to leave the screen door open on a hot summer night, be gone for three or four hours and the only thing that came through the door was the dog.

I wonder what it was like to see snow. Snow that was deep, white with no soot or dust on it at all.

I wonder what it felt like to drive across that old covered bridge. It was a hundred years old, but always held up. It may have creaked, but you always got across.

I wonder what it must've been like to see Mother and Dad *together* laughing and smiling.

I wonder what it was like to ride on a streetcar.

I wonder what it must've been like to wear corduroy knickers and high tops with a knife in the boot.

I wonder what it was like to hear a newspaper boy holler, "Extra, extra!" What it must have been like, that first kiss. (I can tell you what it must've been like because I remember, I was there.)

Is it still there? The creek, the fields, the people, the bridge? I don't know. Probably some are, some aren't.

Is it a sign of old age to be saying, "What it must've been like"? No, there were good times and sad times. What it must've been like? Thank God, I can remember! I lived it all and saw what it must've been like growing up. I think I'm still growing up; I know I'm still a little boy.

You know, I wonder what it must've been like to be in my mother's womb for nine long months. I wonder what it must've been like for her? What *that* must've been like. Well, I confess I don't think any of us can tell you that. I just hope I didn't cause her too much discomfort. I think all the pain came for both of us after I was born.

WAR PAINT

In the past my great-grandfather wore war paint when he rode against the Long Knives (the U.S. Cavalry), and so it was with my grandfather. But my father wore war paint only during ceremonial dances and when the medicine man of the village would summon all for a powwow when a chief died. Many times the tribe would dance for a great bumper crop or for an abundance of rain, for we were always in need of water.

Today, I put on my war paint for the worst enemy I have ever had to face—alcohol. I lined up in front of me the many kinds of drinks I had consumed over the

years: a bottle of bourbon, a bottle of scotch, a bottle
of gin, a bottle of vodka, a bottle of wine and a can
of beer. These had been my enemies since high school
days. How many jails I have been in I couldn't tell
you—far too many. I had lost my driver's license a
couple of years ago. If I had to leave the reservation,
I'd have to sit in the back of my brother's pickup.
I live in a broken-down pueblo on the edge of the
reservation. I can't remember when I held down a real
job. My hands were shaking so badly I couldn't write
or hold papers.

Alcohol has been a terrible problem for the American Indian. True, we are the "first Americans," but
what good is it—we have nothing to show for it. Much
of our land is still being taken away from us—at this
very writing, as a matter of fact. This wasn't why I
drank—I don't know why I drank. But today I decided
it was time for me to quit. I knew that if I didn't, I
would never see forty—I am now thirty-five. I used
to be a good silversmith and a good painter in water-
color and oil.

I placed all the bottles on an old two-by-four a few
feet away from me. Though my hands were shaking
badly, I put the colors on my face. I sat with both
arms over my head and the palms of my hands open.
The tribe's medicine man, Blue Snake, had given me

an old gourd, a sort of rattle to get the attention of the Great Spirit. How long I sat there I can't tell you —maybe as long as six hours. It was sunny and warm when I first sat down and now it was cold and storm clouds were gathering. Strong winds were swirling about me and the bottles. The winds were getting stronger and stronger. The clouds were so black I couldn't see the bottles that were only a few feet away.

Then suddenly the winds subsided—the black clouds were gone and the sun came out. I looked at myself and became aware that I was covered with a thick layer of dust. And then I looked at the bottles— they were all filled with mud.

How many times my mother would speak to me of Mother Earth and Father Sky! Mother Earth was saying, "Drink from the creeks or the rivers; these are the waters that only speak truth—the real truth." One of the bottles had broken and I held up a large piece of glass and I could see my face in the glass. All the dust and rain had not disturbed my war paint. Perhaps my war with alcohol was over—my war paint had paid off. Maybe I couldn't get our land back, I doubt if I could ever be a chief, and it was far too late to be an Olympic medalist, but the one thing I could do was to become one of the tribe's best artists. I went back to my room and got my paints out and began to paint myself, a self-portrait.

Never again would I have to wear war paint, for my biggest war had come to an end.

SHADOWS

What a shadow means to two lovers sitting under a shady tree.

What a shadow means to a scorched, hot desert when a handful of big fluffy clouds drift over it.

A weather vane, old and rusty, casts a small but pretty shadow on an Andrew Wyeth–type barn.

The shadow a huge leaning tree casts over a stream where a few rainbow trout hide momentarily.

The many shadows the flags of various countries cast on the rim of the Olympic Stadium.

The shadows the huge sails cast on the sea as a ship moves slowly across the water.

The shadow an eagle casts. (His shadow is a rare one; therefore his shadow is as important as he is.)

The shadow a mother elephant casts over its young one as they both stand in a watering hole. That has to be a *massive* shadow.

The shadow a cross casts on an unmarked grave in a veterans' cemetery.

The shadow a wide sombrero casts on the bronzed face of a Mexican farm worker as he props himself against the one tree at the end of the field.

The shadow that embraces a pretty lady on a crowded street in Rome, almost making her a Renoir; the shadow covering her is a parasol.

The small shadow of a butterfly landing nervously on a beautiful flower.

All those magnificent shadows, all different at the end of a day in the Grand Canyon.

The shadows of a work gang on a railroad.

The shadows of an Indian chief sitting on his beautiful Appaloosa horse, reenacting a ceremony that the tribe practiced before the white man came.

The shadows all those tall buildings cast on the people in the cities.

The shadows of bars on a mental patient or prisoner, making him look like a zebra standing alone at the zoo.

The shadow a statue of a World War I hero casts

on an old soldier from the same war sitting on a park bench.

The shadow from a trash can that covers the face of a drunk.

The shadows of six men hanging from the gallows, making them appear to be much taller than they are.

A fat lady in the circus, with her shadow alone covering a dozen children staring at her.

A shadow of a light plane as it banks over an old walrus in the Arctic.

The individual shadows of eleven men, football players, standing at attention listening to the singing of "The Star-Spangled Banner."

The ghostlike shadow of the decaying buildings in a onetime boomtown of the Old West.

Factory workers sitting in the shadows of the company's huge smokestacks.

The tiny shadow a newborn baby casts on its mother as it is lifted by the doctor and spanked to bring the first breath.

Tall, old totem poles of British Columbia staring straight ahead, casting lengthy shadows on their viewers.

A grotesque, almost bloody shadow of a freshly killed bull in the bullring in Madrid.

The shadows from a flickering fire as they dance

about and around two lovers stretched on a thick rug in front of it.

As many times as we've all stood in the sunshine, we will all eventually stand in the shadows. Our shadows, do they really belong to us? Are they just visitors from time to time? If the sun doesn't give us shadows, then a full moon will come along once a month and add its shadows. I think if we were ever to talk to our shadows, the night shadows should be the ones. If for no other reason than that they themselves have been waiting all day to cast their shadows.

MY HOBBY

I collect rainbows after a thundershower. (They're rare!) I collect *authentic* winks from beautiful women. I collect warm handshakes from complete strangers. (I'm always, every day and every night, on the look-out for a *smile*.) I collect the sounds of laughter. Not really as plentiful as they used to be.

I collect mean expressions. (I have so many now, I'm ready to trade for other things.) I collect "Thank yous" and phrases like "I'll never forget you," "You've made my day!" I collect postcards with scenes that don't exist anymore. I have a huge collection on pain, but seldom refer to it. Like it or not, it's one heck of a part of my collection. Funny thing about pain, it's hard to trade or unload.

I collect the expressions of kitties or puppies. Wish I could collect that smell that goes along with them. I collect sunsets and sunrises. You say they're always the same? Wrong! I collect the looks of patients in hospitals. Sometimes, I swear, no matter what has happened to them, what their color or sex is, they all seem to look and sound the same.

I feel sorry for people who don't have a hobby, who don't collect anything! How many times have you heard in life: "Why hell, there are a lot of things I'd like to collect, but I can't afford it!" or "I don't have the money, it's as simple as that!"

The one thing we can all collect, the least expensive and perhaps the most rewarding of all: our memories. Have I missed certain things that I should have collected and didn't? Sure! It's the one hobby remaining, the rarest hobby since the beginning! Not one of us can say our collection is complete without it. It's the one thing none of us can find in an antique shop, a gallery, alongside the Nile, off the Great Barrier Reef, at the peak of Everest or at the bottom of the ocean's floor—time!

SUMMER

The birds seem to sing louder and longer and all
nature comes to life,
Bees and wasps busy and buzzing, the sun beating
down,
As you lie on the checkered cloth and roll on the
ground.
And the deviled eggs are out of this world, the
sandwiches disappear
And a hand goes in the cooler for a Coke or a beer.
A time for the lazy, hazy ones who've waited all year
for this,

The young and the old that lie under the maple, the pine, and kiss.

The dog with an infected ear that's covered with flies, whose tongue

Darts in and out as his baleful look is drawn to the skies.

The put-put of the motorboat on its way across the pond,

The splash of the swimmer and then the silhouette as he twists and turns toward the sandy bottom.

The artist paints away, his watercolors out, as he leans forward,

Then sits back upon his camp chair.

And high on a grassy hill sits a young girl combing her stringy but golden hair.

The veterans of many wars sit and talk on the hospital grounds, where the grass is worn and the visitors and patients listen to the Sousa-like sounds.

Amusement parks, the roller coaster and the merry-go-round,

Teenagers in the shooting gallery, a fat woman with two ice cream cones,

A drunk asleep in the Tunnel of Love, a screaming baby stands by a policeman.

By the riverbank a family of blacks wash their car as a white child pulls from the road above a hunk of tar.

The holiday outing, softball, adults and children
   jumping,
Singing and shouting.
The turtle eases his hot shell into the cool, clear water
   and the snake suns himself on the soggy and rotten
   log,
As a bullfrog croaks and a coon from high in a tree
   smiles down at a dog.
Hot, sweaty farmers make their way through rows of
   corn,
Pulling back husks and checking for worms since early
   morn.
The white horses that stand in the field swishing their
   tails
While a group of people throw blackberries in their
   shiny pails.
In the distance a flag is lowered, taps, a boy's camp
   where eyes are closed and so are dreams of the city
As the tenements swelter and Park Avenue apartments
   suddenly become concrete blocks of pity.
Alas the sun, that ball of fire, slips into darkness and
   quietly but quickly the moon makes its way up to
   the stars.
And a sailboat skims across the water, the portable
   plays music

While a couple lying stretched upon her deck gaze
up at Mars.
O Summer, you are one warm blanket we shall never
put away!

MY DEFINITION
OF LOVE

Love starts with a cry, a baby's cry. And then the baby is held and it's loved. Love always ends with a tear.

A little boy or a little girl is loved by both the mother and father. Or the child may be loved by the mother more than the father, or vice versa. Or it may not be loved at all, except by God.

Men of great wealth have given away all their worldly possessions for love, only to never find or receive the love they needed and wanted so badly.

The poor so often have only their love to give, and

when they receive love, it fills them with a richness no wealthy man can understand.

Love is always with us, but so many are afraid to show their feelings. They're so desperately afraid of exposing themselves. Love, true love, does make you terribly vulnerable.

Love is strong and yet it's so terribly delicate—like a fine and rare piece of Venetian glass, it can shatter before your eyes. How many times we're laughed at, for what we share our love with. Our animals, the flowers we look at on a sunny day, birds nesting, an old tree that has stood through three generations, some old toys, photographs of us when we were young, that old attic or basement that's still full of a lot of memories—we loved them all.

I wonder if love, a great and beautiful love, *ever* stops? And if it does, why? And does one have the power to rekindle it, bring it back to what it was?

It's always been fascinating to me that there are so many different kinds of love. Most people love and long for peace. Still others love war. Many—too many —people, love hate, violence, the sight of blood. Some people love to see other people twist and squirm in the presence of others. Many love the real and incredible feeling of touching, holding, of another—of sex.

So many people not only enjoy, but truly love dressing up and pretending they're anybody but who they really are.

People love to be told how much they're loved. There must be a few, I hope only a few, who love to be hated—in fact, thrive on it.

People often speak of "an undying love" for one another. My, what strength lies in that phrase! I wonder if I've known that kind of love?

Is love always with you? Is it always part of you, day in, day out, or does it come and go? It's true I question what true love is all about. Just about the time I think I've found the answer, it slips through my fingers. Real love should be so warm, pleasant, easy, wonderful; then why is there so much pain attached to it?

How much do *you* want to be loved? A lot? Sometimes? A little bit? Till the end of time? Would you love me for *now*? For now is all I'm sure of, *I want to be loved now!*

Don't ever love me when it's convenient. Never hide your love, you just might be a better actress than I bargained for.

Love is only four letters, but maybe someday it will be a bigger word. I think it should be, it's overpowering. I want that word, selfishly, to be huge.

ABOUT THE AUTHOR

JONATHAN WINTERS was born in Dayton, Ohio, in 1925. After serving with the marines in the South Pacific for two and a half years, he studied at Kenyon College and the Dayton Art Institute. Soon thereafter he won a local talent contest, which led to a job as a radio disc jockey. By the mid-fifties, he had moved from the airwaves to the stage, becoming a staple at nightclubs throughout America. Regular television appearances followed, notably on the Garry Moore and Steve Allen shows, and especially on Jack Paar's programs for NBC. His own TV series, *The Jonathan Winters Show*, first aired in 1956. As an actor, Winters has starred in such acclaimed films as *It's a Mad, Mad, Mad, Mad World*, *The Russians Are Coming, the Russians Are Coming, Oh Dad, Poor Dad* and Tony Richardson's classic *The Loved One*, as well as the popular television series *Mork and Mindy*. Today, he continues to make frequent television and motion picture appearances, performs solo concerts, shows his paintings and drawings in galleries throughout the country and is writing his autobiography. He has two grown children and lives with his wife, Eileen, in Los Angeles.